"This is a truly creative and engaging book. Like Goldratt's *The Goal*, this book teaches the principles and concepts that form the basis for effective management of operations through the medium of stories. Learning is fun and painless and yet the lessons are deep."

— **Morris Cohen**
Panasonic Professor of Manufacturing & Logistics,
Co-Director, Fishman-Davidson Center
for Service and Operations Management,
The Wharton School, University of Pennsylvania

"What a great book—so inviting, interesting, and creative. Great practical Lean insights from a non-manufacturing point of view."

— **Professor Arthur V. Hill**
Associate Dean for MBA Programs, The John & Nancy Lindahl
Professor of Supply Chain & Operations and Director,
Supply Chain & Operations Board of Advisors
at Carlson School of Management, University of Minnesota;
Academic Director, Carlson Consulting Enterprise

"Goldberg and Weiss take key business concepts and make them accessible for anyone committed to self-improvement. Their approach is simple and effective...and reminds me how much more I can do to apply Lean thinking both in & out of the office for real results!"

— **Kevin Klau**
Senior Vice President, Business Units, Hach Company

"*The Lean Anthology* is full of rich nuggets of gold that can be applied to both personal and professional life. Rebecca Goldberg and Elliott Weiss have taken a unique approach combining storytelling and teaching through short vignettes that will revolutionize the reader's thinking and lead to lasting business results bolstering your company's competitive advantage. This pragmatic approach is certain to transform you, your team, and those around you"

— **Monica Barker**
Director Strategic Marketing North America, AREVA, Inc.

"Even experienced practitioners can use *The Lean Anthology* to see additional applications for Lean tools. This book is comprehensive, enlightening, refreshing, and fun to read—which allows the reader to easily follow the pragmatic presentation of each lean concept and practice."

— Frederick S. Buchman
Co-Author of Balanced Scorecard Strategies for Dummies,
*2007 and 2008; and President and CEO, Hayward Enterprises Inc.,
senior partner of the Balanced Business Institute*

"Must-reading for anyone with responsibility for or interest in any form of operations. Few managers understand and embrace the importance of continuous improvement. The challenge is to learn how to do it... this is the need this book fulfills."

— Wallace Stettinius
*former Chairman and CEO, Cadmus Communications
Corporation, author of* Principles of General Management,
The Art and Science of Getting Results Across Organizational
Boundaries *and* How to Plan and Execute Strategy: 24
Steps to Implement Any Corporate Strategy Successfully

THE LEAN ANTHOLOGY

A Practical Primer in Continual Improvement

Rebecca Goldberg • **Elliott N. Weiss**

Illustrations by **Michael Twery**

CRC Press
Taylor & Francis Group
Boca Raton   London   New York

CRC Press is an imprint of the
Taylor & Francis Group, an **informa** business

A PRODUCTIVITY PRESS BOOK

CRC Press
Taylor & Francis Group
6000 Broken Sound Parkway NW, Suite 300
Boca Raton, FL 33487-2742

Printed on acid-free paper
Version Date: 20141007

International Standard Book Number-13: 978-1-4822-4679-7 (Paperback)

Library of Congress Cataloging-in-Publication Data

Goldberg, Rebecca.
  The Lean Anthology : a practical primer in continual improvement / Rebecca Goldberg, Elliott Weiss.
      pages cm
  Includes bibliographical references and index.
  ISBN 978-1-4822-4679-7 (pbk. : alk. paper) 1. Lean manufacturing. 2. Production control. 3. Cost control. 4. Quality control. 5. Industrial management. I. Title.

TS155.A1G65 2015
658--dc23   2014034194

Visit the Taylor & Francis Web site at
http://www.taylorandfrancis.com

and the CRC Press Web site at
http://www.crcpress.com

To Alec, Bob, David, Elliott, Emily, Greg, Jeanne, Jimmy, Melissa, Mike, Richard, Tom, Venkat, and Wally for their support of my career, the great conversations, and the many opportunities with which I have been provided over the past six years. In particular, I would like to thank Elliott for his patience. I am forever grateful.

—Rebecca

To Jan Dorman, the love of my life, for continued encouragement and support. It's finally done!

—Elliott

CONTENTS

PART II CAPABILITY

INTRODUCTION

Living Lean: A Practical Primer in Continuous Improvement is a collection of everyday stories about the Lean process improvement journey. The stories are easy-to-understand, simple accounts of everyday people negotiating life. The characters observe and integrate the principles of Lean into their personal and professional lives. This format benefits readers without a manufacturing background—as well as those with a manufacturing background—by presenting information in a familiar context and by extending Lean beyond business settings. Since these stories describe real situations, they are holistic in nature. The scenario and dialogue might incorporate lessons about several topics; however, a primary lesson is revealed in each.

Our definition of Lean is *the relentless pursuit of creating value by strategically eliminating waste*. Each *Lean Anthology* story describes a complete, real-life setting in which one or several Lean principles or tools are explored and then applied to achieve a desired outcome from a leadership point of view. The stories help the reader to understand and intuitively apply a different approach to the strategic elimination of waste as part of a plan for saving money, generating revenues, or freeing up resources. These resources might include time, money, or something else.

A SIMPLE FRAMEWORK: THE 5 CS

Our underlying framework for leading a Lean journey can increase an individual's effectiveness as a consultant, business leader, entrepreneur, or family member. This framework is defined by the tasks and challenges of operating settings. We categorize them as follows:

- **Customer:** Understand the user-defined value proposition.
- **Capability:** Develop the ability to deliver on organizational and individual promises.
- **Control:** Measure and improve processes, services, and products.
- **Coordination:** Work with suppliers and customers along the entire value chain.
- **Context and culture:** Recognize the environment within which the organization is operating, including competitive forces, the culture of the organization, industry dynamics, and the global economic environment.

While the framework begins with the customer value proposition, we emphasize that these steps represent a cycle. While the *customer* step is listed first, one must first consider the final step—*context*—within which the business will operate. The *context and culture* of an environment help identify the *customer* requirements guiding the design of the operations. These requirements directly influence decisions about process *capability* in the areas of cost, quality, delivery, flexibility, innovation, and information. *Control* systems such as workforce planning, inventory monitoring, and scheduling are put in place to optimize the effective deployment of the firm's resources.

Managing internal processes, however, is not sufficient by itself; *coordination* with external entities such as suppliers and customers throughout the entire supply chain is also required for success. We then return full circle to reconsidering the *context*, which has undoubtedly changed, and then shift again to understanding the *customer* and designing processes and systems that deliver distinctive customer value.

The stories in this book are organized into these five sets of concepts. The 5 Cs framework represents five stages of strategic operations design and improvement:

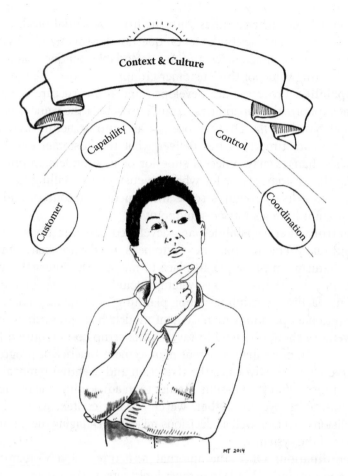

1. **Customer:** The order-winning criteria (OWC) and customer-defined value proposition are identified first. The firm or individual must determine what the current and potential customers want to buy and are willing to pay for. OWC are often categorized as cost, quality, speed, flexibility, innovation, and information. These are linked to who the customer is, what the customer's behavior "looks like," and what the customer needs. The value proposition should be defined with an eye to the customer's current product or services and the degree of familiarity that the

potential customer base has with the firm's potential product or service offering. The fundamental question for this step is "What are my core competencies and my defendable, unique potential for creating value for this customer group?"

2. **Capability:** Processes are developed and infrastructure is built that supports the capabilities required to deliver the value proposition *based on the OWC*. Processes and infrastructure may be altered over time to better deliver what the customer expects. These changes may reflect a superior or new understanding of who the customer is or for what the customer is willing to pay. This stage likely requires some investment of resources and is important from a strategic standpoint.

3. **Control:** After capabilities are developed, organizations must continually ensure that the customer's needs are being met. Mechanisms must be put in place to manage the internal organizational systems. These systems include inventory management, facility scheduling, labor planning, and quality control. Traditional operations management models have prescribed that inventory should be held to save on the setup costs required for production of an item. Current management practice at progressive companies advocates the reduction and eventual removal of inventory wherever possible. Rather than advocating one of these philosophies over the other, we emphasize context as the key decision driver, as well as decisions related to *changing* the parameters of the system.

4. **Coordination:** Once the internal structures of an organization are optimized, a leader must look outside the organization, both upstream (to suppliers) and downstream (to customers), in order to best *coordinate* the end-to-end functioning of the system. *Coordination* deals with the systems, tasks, and decisions involving the relationship between manufacturing or service organizations and their customers and suppliers. The versatility of the supply chain is a critical component of a firm's competitive advantage in today's marketplace. Operating decisions within a coordination context may include vendor selection, just-in-time purchasing relationships, global plant location and distribution decisions, production scheduling, and distribution network

design. The operations manager needs to consider many factors when making such decisions, such as the location and availability of inexpensive skilled labor, the length of the distribution pipeline, transportation costs, political and foreign exchange risk, tax considerations, and operating capabilities.

5. **Context:** The *context* of a business or individual is what drives each of the previous four steps in the strategic development and execution of an operations design. The *context* includes both internal and external stakeholders. External stakeholders might include investors, suppliers, distributors, customers, the media, and governing or regulating bodies. Internal stakeholders might include private investors, employees, and partners. Competition must also be considered.

All these stories contain some element of context evaluation, because each is a real-world example. Each character is driven by some context-dependent need to create the change that they seek. In the business world, a context analysis might also focus on competitive forces, such as new entrants, barriers to entry, the power of suppliers and consumers, and available substitutions.

Understanding and taking advantage of Lean principles, whether in a personal or business context, can mean the difference between taking a reactive approach (How can I remove the issue I am facing *right now*?) and a proactive position (As I address this problem, how can I take steps to build capability for the future?). The latter, proactive approach requires a leadership perspective and the strategic application of a set of tools and principles like those described in this book.

Since the 5 Cs business development framework is cyclical, there is an opportunity to improve with each new set of circumstances. For instance, a leader could use information gained while defining the *customer* value proposition to inform the *capability* and *control* development process. Then, the insights gained in the *coordination* step can improve engagement with the organization's *context* (markets, stakeholders, and competition) to gather additional insights about the current climate. A better understanding of *context* can then be used to refine the organization's value proposition for its *customers*, continuing the cycle.

HOW TO USE THIS BOOK

As you read these stories about Lean, give some thought to any parallels you notice in your own life, whether on a personal or professional level. The purpose of this book is to help you discover new ways of improving your personal and professional processes. Each story begins with a brief summary and a suggested focus for your reading. The questions provided will help you place the story within a context for deeper understanding.

An explanation is provided after each story that highlights key concepts for an operations manager involved in continuous process improvement or Lean transformation. Study questions are provided that help you frame the learnings. Each chapter also contains a section called "Brain Play" to help extend your learning to other contexts.

The stories are organized along the 5 Cs framework, and they may be read in that order. Although some concepts build upon previous chapters, the stories can also be read independently, or selected by Lean concepts or business or personal concepts of interest.

ACKNOWLEDGMENTS

The authors would like to thank those people who provided situational context for the stories, including Todd Pearson, Erika Deibert, David Dube, Tracy Scott, Bob Liebe, Kate McKone, Brian Venuti, Peter Wilbert, Zeke Weiss, Jackson Oliver, and Wyatt Oliver. Kevin Klau and Ray Butler of Danaher Corporation introduced Elliott to the practical aspects of Lean. We would also like to thank those who gave us feedback for previous versions of this book, including John Leschke, Donald Stevenson, Steve Momper, Lia Norton, Leslie Mullin, and Beth Woods. The Darden School of the University of Virginia and Alec Horniman provided us with the resources and intellectual environment to make the book possible. Thanks also to our families and friends for supporting us and encouraging us though this venture.

ABOUT THE AUTHORS

Rebecca Goldberg is a strategy and operations consultant with more than a decade of experience. She has extensively published articles and case studies in the *Washington Post, Bloomberg Businessweek, Business & Economy*, and in the University of Virginia and Columbia University case collections. She writes in the areas of strategy, operations, and technology life cycles, as well as in negotiation, team dynamics, and collaboration. She has consulted with significant global clients in a variety of industries, including health care delivery, pharmaceuticals, consumer goods, integrated technology solutions, professional  services, insurance, and the military. She holds an MBA from the Darden School of Business; a BA from Tufts University, magna cum laude with highest thesis honors; and a BFA from the School of the Museum of Fine Arts, Boston. She lives in Richmond, Virginia, with her two sons.

Elliott N. Weiss is the Oliver Wight Professor of Business Administration at the Darden School of Business at the University of Virginia. Weiss teaches in the operations area and is the author of numerous articles in the areas of production management and operations research; he has extensive consulting experience, for both manufacturing and service companies, in the areas of production scheduling, workflow management, logistics, total productive maintenance, and Lean implementation. He is the author of over 175 cases and technical notes in the area of operations management.

Before coming to Darden in 1987, Weiss was on the faculty of the Johnson Graduate School of Management at Cornell University. He has held visiting appointments at the Graduate School of Management at the University of Melbourne, Australia, and at the Wharton School of the University of Pennsylvania.

He is married with four children and one grandchild.

About the Artist

Michael Twery grew up in Lynchburg, Virginia. He studied at the Rhode Island School of Design and the San Francisco Art Institute, where he received his BFA & MFA degrees in Painting. Michael has worked as an artist-in-residence and art instructor for over 25 years and exhibited work for over 35 years. He currently works out of his studio in downtown Lynchburg doing commissions and creating new bodies of work. He may be contacted through his website mtartspace.com<**http://mtartspace.com**>.

PART I

Customer

CHAPTER 1

Defining the Customer Value Proposition

THERON HUNTER'S COFFEE SHOP

Planning to shelve his corporate career and open a high-end coffeehouse, Theron Hunter meets with his friend and potential business partner, John Perucci, to discuss his options. He identifies his target market and ideal location, then considers factors relevant to creating value for professional daytime foot traffic.

As you read Theron's story, think about what Theron needs to do to make his coffee shop appealing enough to potential customers. What choices must he make in order to become profitable? How should he decide among the alternatives?

Theron Hunter was a coffee man. He had been going to the annual National Coffee Association conferences since 1993. He loved the countless varietals of coffee beans and savored the subtle differences caused by climate, soil composition, and farming methods as would a true wine connoisseur. He also had become involved in the fair trade and sustainable harvest movements before the chain coffee retailers did. It had been Theron's lifelong dream to open up a successful coffee shop that embraced the richness and diversity of flavor that he knew could be expressed through the perfectly brewed cup.

After a 20-year stint as a banker in Washington, DC, Theron decided he would begin working on a plan to transition out of his day job and invest most of his savings into opening a coffee shop of his own. His vision for the coffee shop was not that of a large-chain coffee shop, which relied on expansion, duplication, quality, and consistency to support the bottom line. Theron's model was different; he simply wanted to own one coffee shop, but he wanted that one single shop to be world class.

After a great deal of thought about location and the cost of rent, he determined that the best place for him to locate his world-class destination would be on Capitol Hill. Though the trendy location and high-end buildout would be pricey, he believed this was where he needed to be to make his endeavor a success. Here was his market; now he just had to figure out how to serve it.

What were the criteria that his future customers would use to evaluate his establishment? While the average Joe who would walk past his front door would appreciate the quality and variety he was interested in serving, that same average person did not have much time. And brewing individual cups would take time. Theron decided to talk over his value proposition with his trusted friend and potential business partner, John Perucci. One night after work, at the Old Ebbitt Grill, located across from the White House, they ordered martinis and a large selection from the raw bar. Theron and John admired the massive plate of delectable seafood on ice as it was served to them on a chilled stand. After a few bites, they got down to business.

Theron: So, what do you think about my coffee shop?

John: Well, I think it has to make money. Otherwise it's an expensive hobby, and your wife is going to get mad at you for spending all your savings on a hobby. Besides, I know you like your seafood.

Theron: Good point. Well, I'm going to have to make it a world-class coffee shop, then.

John: How are you going to do that? You're a banker, not a restaurant owner. Just because you sign a lease with a massive monthly price tag and spend a lot of money on decorations doesn't mean you'll make money. You make money by providing goods or services that people want to buy and can afford. And let's face it: you don't have the buying power of a large chain of coffee shops. How are you going to compete?

Theron: My idea is to provide a better selection. You know, 39 flavors or something. Freshly ground, organic, fair trade, in a selection that people haven't been exposed to before.

John: But the foot traffic in the area you're considering doesn't have that much time. You might be better off with only a few choices and a fast wait in the line.

Theron: Yes, I thought of that. You have to make a clear choice about what you're offering, don't you? Speed, cost, quality, or customization—you can't have it all. You have to focus on one or two.

John: You clearly can't be offering breaks on cost. You're going to have to charge the highest price the market will bear, and offer quality instead. You just have to decide whether your secondary value proposition will be speed or customization. It sounds like you really want to offer the customization, but that the market may value speed more. And they can get that at a chain coffee shop. So I still don't see how you're going to compete. If your only point of differentiation is that you're an independent coffee shop, I don't think you're going to make it. A potential customer needs to clearly see the benefit of choosing your store over another one. And the benefit has to be to them, not to you. No offense, but no one cares about you!

Theron: I know you're right, but I really want to find a way to make this work. It's my *dream*. Hey—what if I offer both? A customer who gets in one line can order quickly from one of two large thermal carafes of coffee. That line has little or no variety— just a bold or medium blend. Someone who's in a rush can get in and out in under 2 minutes. The barista brews another pot every time the levels get low. Meanwhile, customers get a chance to look over the custom selection, and they come back when they have the time to try a new flavor.

The other line can be for people who have more time to stay and enjoy their cup, and they can choose from the 39 flavors. The barista would dispense just the right amount of beans into a grinder, put the grounds into a French press or drip station, and put a big mug right under that. So in this case, the coffee doesn't get made until it's ordered and paid for, and it takes longer—the customization is part of the experience. If you're staying to drink it, you're willing to wait, right?

John: Well, you're also going to have to consider the cost of rent on the Hill. If you're offering tables, you need a restroom. You need to think about your cost per square foot. Some of those carts on the street might be making more money because their rent is so much less. Smaller delis that don't offer seating might have a bigger profit margin. World class is hard to achieve, my friend.

Theron: Well, think about this. I could easily offer prepackaged yogurts, sandwiches, and fruit plates with the coffee, which would increase my per-customer receipt. But in addition, I could offer a similar type of light fare in the evening, and the coffee shop could double as a wine bar! I wouldn't have to pay an evening chef and a waitstaff if the customers ordered from the same counter where the coffee is sold.

John: Wine costs way more per glass than coffee does. You'd have crossover traffic from both sets of customers: people who come in to share happy hour with a group might take a look at your custom coffee setup and decide to return to sample your brews the next day. I could see you making that work. You could take advantage of the same foot traffic twice: coffee in the morning, happy hour in the evening. You wouldn't even have to stay open that late, maybe 8:00 p.m. Now you've got me thinking. Let me talk to a few folks, and I'll get back to you.

THE VALUE PROPOSITION
OF THE COFFEE SHOP

VALUE PROPOSITION

Lean Takeaways

In order to identify those activities that do not add value, one must first understand the customer-defined value proposition. Only when one realizes how cost, quality, delivery, and customization are important to the customer can one take steps to improve the product, service, or experience. Thus, for Theron, to "lean out" his coffee shop and remove waste, he must first define this value for the customer.

Future stories will address sources of this waste and activities involved in identifying and removing it.

The *value proposition* is a clear description of the value a seller provides to a buyer. It is *always* defined from the point of view of the buyer and not from the point of view of the seller. As John points out, some of the value that Theron proposes, such as fair trade, organic, high-quality coffee, and an independent shop as opposed to a franchise, will benefit customers only if the price is right. Since this potential coffee shop will be costly to rent and maintain, any value perceived by the consumer must be at a cost he or she is willing to pay. Businesses face the challenge of creating a valuable match between what can be produced and what the intended market will want to consume.

ORDER-WINNING CRITERIA

Six criteria might win a customer's order: cost, quality, speed, flexibility (customization), innovation, and information. Historically, manufacturers and service providers choose one or two of these dimensions on which to compete. Consider the auto-shop sign that reads, "We do three types of jobs, good, cheap and quick. Good and cheap won't be quick; cheap and quick won't be good; and good and quick won't be cheap." Current competitive realities, however, are forcing consideration of three or four of these criteria simultaneously.

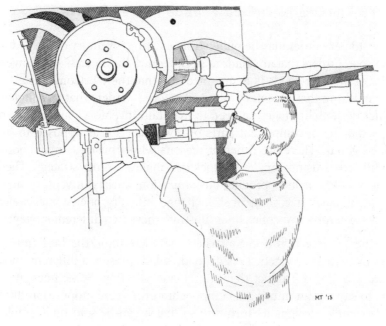

WHILE TWO OUT OF THREE MAY HAVE BEEN GOOD AT ONE TIME,
CUSTOMERS CURRENTLY DEMAND ALL THREE.

Theron's two different coffee lines take these dimensions of *order-winning criteria* (OWC) into consideration. The first queue offers only two options (bold or medium) and is priced at a premium but moves quickly and offers products of high quality. The second queue offers an extensive array of customized products—also high-quality products sold at a premium—but moves slowly due to the trade-off between speed and customization.

Businesses face this decision when deciding how their product should be positioned in the market. One example is real estate. In any given city, the price paid for a property will reflect some adjustment based on quality, customization, and required transaction speed. A transaction that a seller wants to occur quickly might result in the loss of negotiating power. A second seller might prioritize being able to recoup the maximum amount of equity and be willing to wait for a full-price offer. A third seller might be a builder who customizes new homes by pricing out special extras separately. The buyer must wait for these to be completed and will pay more for them.

MAKE TO ORDER VERSUS MAKE TO STOCK

A customer's order may be pulled from existing inventory or created on the spot. Orders that are *made to stock* require that at least some inventory of finished goods is maintained and that there be some means of replenishing that inventory, often in batches. Orders that are *made to order* do not eliminate the need to maintain inventory, but the inventory may be of component parts or raw materials, as opposed to finished goods. There are different reasons why a business may choose to fill orders using a make-to-stock or a make-to-order strategy. These reasons may include product customization, variety, inventory management, batch size, setup or shift change difficulty, or customer preferences. Theron's two coffee lines illustrate these two different strategies.

Businesses face this decision when they determine the best time to assemble their products. Freshly made salads present a different, more luxury-oriented product than a premade selection. Sometimes, making to stock is an important component of the value proposition. Ikea, for example, designs its furniture so that it can be sold unassembled in flat boxes that are easy to pack, ship, or transport in or on top of a vehicle. Providing products as space-efficient, stackable, inventory-friendly kits is an intentional make-to-stock decision that is part of Ikea's value proposition. Custom-made furniture crafted by a skilled carpenter is at the other end of the spectrum. The customer gets exactly what is wanted but must wait for construction and delivery.

VOICE OF THE CUSTOMER

What insights can we gain from Theron and John's conversation about opening a coffee shop that can help us understand the following:

- Customer-defined value proposition?
- Order-winning criteria?
- Make to order versus make to stock?
- Voice of the customer?
- Competing on capabilities?
- Operating system strategic design?

As with the value proposition and the OWC, the *voice of the customer* (VOC) emphasizes the customer's point of view. The VOC can be "heard" through passive observation or active engagement. Data collection at point of sale or via analysis of social media trending would be considered passive, since the customer is not intentionally participating. Surveys, focus groups, or direct responses to blogs or Twitter feeds are a more active form of engaging with customers.

Theron cannot conduct research with customers he does not yet have, but he considers the VOC when he thinks critically about his value proposition and OWC. VOC conversations allow a business to leverage customers as partners and build a rapport that can mitigate the inevitable crisis or mistake. Lean involves going to the *gemba*, the source, in order to see how a product or service is produced, delivered, or consumed. Only by "going to see" can the organization understand its true value proposition.

COMPETING ON CAPABILITIES

Competing on capabilities means that a company considers what it has to offer that is unique and defensible (e.g., high barriers to entry, specialized knowledge or access to capital, equipment, or other resources) and uses this knowledge to help define its value proposition. John encourages Theron to consider the VOC, but he must also consider his own core capabilities. An effective value proposition balances the two, leveraging the things that the business does very well in service of what customers want.

Theron has an expert knowledge of coffee, which is a unique capability he wants to leverage. Established companies tend to leverage capabilities such as distribution channels, negotiated contracts with suppliers, manufacturing capability, or intellectual capabilities. When IBM became disconnected with the VOC, for example, it was still selling and servicing large mainframes as the business world moved to distributed systems. As a result, it almost went bankrupt. But it had retained enough specialized knowledge, customer relationships, high-investment equipment, R&D experience, and other capabilities to restructure itself as a service company providing customized data management solutions. By identifying and competing on its considerable capabilities, IBM managed to reclaim a portion of the market.

OPERATING SYSTEM STRATEGIC DESIGN

An operating system is designed strategically when it is aligned with each of the above concepts. When Theron envisions the dual-line system and considers when the large thermal carafes of coffee will be refilled, he is aligning systems strategically. When he considers the location of the restrooms and that customers in the express line must somehow negotiate space with customers in the slower lines, he starts to consider issues of space layout. Ideally, Theron would think critically and continuously about each operating system decision.

BRAIN PLAY

- How do each of Theron's operating system decisions affect his value proposition? Which are most critical to his business' success?
- How might an ice cream parlor use the concepts of make to stock or make to order? A clothing manufacturer?
- What is your personal value proposition? What are the skills that you bring or might bring to your current or future organization? How is this similar to Theron's situation? How is it different?

CHAPTER 2

Managing Variability

LUNCH WITH GUINEVERE

Chloe Adams attempts to enjoy a peaceful lunch at a high-end hotel restaurant with her old college friend Jennifer Anderson—and she has brought along her toddler, Guinevere. The waitstaff flexes their operational muscles and pulls out all the stops to provide excellent customer service for both the two friends with an infant and the rest of the diners.

As you read about lunch with Guinevere, think about the choices that the Walden-Aster Hotel has made to enhance Chloe and Jennifer's experience. What operational decisions have they made to support their approach?

Charles, maître d' of the restaurant at the Walden-Aster Hotel, hears an animated exchange echo among the chandeliers, then sees two women walk across the lobby, one pushing a stroller. Of the two reservations for two people at noon— both under the name Jennifer—one, he knows, has already checked in, so he surmises this is the other.

In the stroller, a toddler in a pink-and-black frock twists left and right to look at the vaulted Beaux Arts ceilings. As her mother begins unbuckling her, Charles approaches them and gestures to the stroller.

Charles: Three for lunch, ladies? May I set this aside for you?
Chloe: Oh, if I could get a high chair, that would be great.

In a single motion, Charles collapses the stroller and hands it to Gustaf, the busboy; as Charles shows Jennifer, Chloe, and Chloe's daughter to their table, Gustaf silently reappears with a high chair and some teething biscuits for the daughter, Guinevere.

Charles: Your server, Wink, will be right with you. Thank you for joining us this afternoon.

Charles's thinking is that in order to provide the best service possible to all the guests in the dining room, the staff should be apprised of the toddler's presence, so he relays the information to John, the executive chef of lunch, before returning to his post. John takes the information to the kitchen.

John: There's a small child at table 13.
Lucky: [*sous chef, lunch*]: Yes, chef.
John: Who has that table?
Wink: I got it.

As Wink, the senior server of the shift, moves to take the ladies'
drink orders, Lucky and John reassess their position. How behind are
their custom orders, and what does their inventory look like on critical ingredients?

MT '11

Lucky: We're fine; stocked up on everything.
John: But we're starting to back up now, with peak an hour off. Let's fill
the orders right away as they come in.
Lucky: I'm down to 3 minutes each on the chef's special and 9 minutes
on anything custom.
John: Perfect. But the backup is coming, and on top of that, the better
you keep the salad bar stocked, the more likely another guest
will select it, freeing you up to prep chef's specials and cus-
tom orders from the menu.
Lucky: Look at this: half a dozen orders up while we've been talking.
Let me know what Wink brings back.
John: I'll help you get caught up before table 13's order comes in.
Lucky: Yes, chef. Thanks.

Several of the orders are chef's specials, which can be prepared simultaneously using fewer motions. Lucky takes those plates while John focuses on the custom orders from the menu. Meanwhile, at table 13, Wink takes the orders.

Wink [*pouring water from a carafe before setting it on the table*]: Something from the wine cellar this afternoon?

Jennifer: I'd love a glass of that nice white we sampled last week—the one with a lobster on the front?

Chloe: That sounds intriguing.

Wink: The '09 Lobster Reef Sauvignon Blanc. Would you care for a bottle today?

Chloe [*glancing at Jennifer, who smiles*]: Oh, we'd better stick to a glass each, thanks.

Wink: I'll be right back with your drinks.

Guinevere, who has dropped a biscuit between her legs, struggles with the high chair straps and begins to whine at a volume that seems to reach the lobby. Chloe glances at the other diners, but none look up. Wink returns quickly with the wine and begins to describe the restaurant's lunch offerings.

Wink: There are three options for lunch, ladies, as your schedule permits [*glances at Guinevere and smiles*]: a selection from the menu takes 15 to 20 minutes. The chef's special today is she-crab soup with a tossed salad and a fresh egg beignet, which takes a third of the time. Or, if you prefer, you may help yourself to our salad bar.

Jennifer: She-crab soup all around.
Chloe: The baby and I will share.
Wink: Excellent.

The women barely have time to taste the wine when Wink returns with a beignet for Guinevere, who becomes completely absorbed in dissecting the impossibly light, stretchy layers of dough. The women return to their conversation.

Jennifer: What do you do when she cries?
Chloe [sighs deeply]: When she really needs to, we get up and leave. But she slept well last night, and I try to do this often enough so we can take a chance on outings like this, when you want to share a nice experience with them.

Wink brings the ladies their salads, explosions of endive and radicchio, as Guinevere continues to deconstruct the beignet. It is a perfect moment.

MT '11

MANAGING VARIABILITY IN LUNCH ORDERS AT THE WALDEN-ASTER

ACCOMMODATING VARIABILITY IN DEMAND

There are three ways to accommodate a given level of variability of demand:

1. Inventory
2. Capacity
3. Lead time

Any one of the three options can replace the other two. Customer orders can be (1) fulfilled from a make-to-stock strategy using inventory, (2) fulfilled from a make-to-order strategy using capacity, or (3) fulfilled by having customers wait using lead time. Make to order and make to stock are two options for filling customer orders that have been described in the story entitled "Theron Hunter's Coffee Shop" (Chapter 1). The Walden-Aster's dining room makes menu and chef's special items to order, and it stocks up the salad bar as a make-to-stock option that allows customers to build their own salads in a shorter time period. The salad bar is actually a form of "delayed customization" or "postponement" that combines the use of make to stock and make to order.

Lean Takeaways

One key category of waste is inventory. But holding inventory is also one important strategy for managing variability in customer demand. Lead time and capacity are other levers for reducing the effect of variability in customer demand. Lean implementations look for ways to manage this variability in order to decrease the need for inventory, capacity, or lead time.

In this chapter, we examine strategies for managing when confronted with variability; in Chapter 3, we will look at the ways in which inventory impacts wait time. In future chapters, we will examine ways to reduce variability and its many impacts.

Delayed customization is an approach that prepares a product up to a certain point in the value chain (partially completed items are made to stock) and completes the production process only after the specific order arrives (made to order or assembled to order). One example is a restaurant serving coffee and sandwiches. The coffee may be prepared in a pot, but the customer will customize it by adding the desired amounts of milk, cream, or sweeteners. Sandwich ingredients may be prepared in advance, but the final product is made only after the customer places an order. This approach allows for more variety and less inventory, since component parts may be used in many different final products. By leveling the workload (i.e., performing work in advance), the inventory of made-to-stock items also frees up capacity to handle demand variability.

Below, we look at the three options in more detail.

INVENTORY

Inventory can be thought of in many ways: as a stockpile of raw materials, a quantity of partially finished materials, or a store of finished goods. A floorboard mill shop, for instance, might purchase raw hardwood trees from South Carolina and truck them in on flatbeds. The shop receives the trees and immediately sets about running the tree trunks through a machine to remove the bark. Next, it planes the wood and creates boards of the proper dimensions. The wood is run through a mechanical sander and cut to size. Last, the floorboards are pre-stained and sealed, since this company sells ready-to-install floorboards. However, the company does not bundle the stacks together for shipment until an order is placed. All of these stages are considered work-in-process inventory until the stacks are bundled, and then the stacks are considered finished-goods inventory.

The point in a process where work-in-process inventory is held is a strategic decision that has to do with offering the most value to the customer. John and Lucky, who run the kitchen at the Walden-Aster, busily chop tomatoes and shred cheese to prepare for the onslaught of the lunch rush hour. Why did they not purchase chopped tomatoes, or shred the cheese the night before? Because the taste is not as flavorful when tomatoes are not freshly chopped, and the Walden-Aster is a high-end establishment with the highest of gastronomic standards. They chop and shred their whole, unprocessed foods less than an hour in advance to maximize aroma, texture, and flavor. The chopped tomatoes and shredded cheese are then considered partially completed "work-in-process" inventory. Ingredients prepared in advance—especially for custom-menu items—can preserve kitchen capacity during peak times.

CAPACITY

Capacity is the amount of product or service that can be produced in a given period of time. Its units are measured in pieces per time period or services per time period. The capacity of a snack chip factory is the quantity of packaged bags of chips that can be produced within a given time period. The factory is a system that might be constrained by equipment, people, processes, external factors, or other factors.

The capacity of a pharmaceutical-manufacturing facility, as another example, might be defined as "3 million pain-relieving capsules each quarter." If that pharmaceutical-manufacturing facility can theoretically produce 3 million capsules per quarter, this does not mean that this many capsules are actually produced. It only means that this is the *capacity* of the facility. A portion of that capacity may be used, and another portion considered *idle*. Idle capacity is a resource that represents the investments that a company has made in its capacity to produce finished goods—such as capital equipment purchases, employee hiring and training, and facility overhead. It is a resource that is more explicitly time-based than other resources such as capital and real estate because it disappears if it is not used.

John and Lucky in the dining room use the capacity of the kitchen to fill customer lunch orders. Lucky can assemble only a certain number of custom-menu items per hour at his peak capacity—but, prior to the lunchtime rush, a portion of his time is spent idle. He can, therefore, make better use of his time by assembling some chef's specials in the hour prior to the rush. The lunch rush is the period when Lucky's time will be utilized "at capacity." John also pitches in and uses some of *his* time to help Lucky prepare some chef's specials in advance. In doing so, John contributes capacity to the total system. By building inventory ahead of time, extra capacity is made available at times of peak demand. This strategic use of capacity effectively increases the number of meals that can be produced without extending customer wait times.

The capacity of a system can also be a function of the product mix. Consider a doughnut shop. Its capacity may be 30,000 glazed doughnuts per week, yet the same machinery may be able to make only 20,000 cream-filled, chocolate doughnuts. The leadership of the doughnut company may determine that it is more important, from a broader business strategy standpoint, to produce more of one type of doughnut than another.

What can Jennifer, Chloe, and Guinevere's experience teach us about the concepts of managing demand variability through:

The use of inventory?
The use of capacity?
The use of lead time?

LEAD TIME

Lead time is defined as the length of time between the moment an order is placed to the moment the order is filled. Some variability in lead time is expected. Even orders that are filled via computer technology are subject to external forces and variability. In many cases, the greater the human interaction portion of the process, the greater the variability. Lead time is a function of the available capacity and the inventory in the system. If goods or services are provided from inventory (i.e., make to stock), then lead time may be minimal. If capacity and inventory are unavailable at the time a good or service is demanded (i.e., make to order), the lead time will be extended.

Lucky runs his kitchen so effectively that, assuming there is capacity in the system, he has a good idea of the amount of time required to fill either a chef's special or a custom-menu item. The lead times are different, because the chef's special is prepped mostly in advance, while the lead times for custom-menu items depend on the number of orders in line during the lunchtime rush. Without careful management of his systems, Lucky might find that his lead time stretches out unacceptably, and he leaves angry customers waiting for their food.

Lucky can only work on one custom plate at a time. He pays attention to his processes, and he does his best to minimize the variability of his lead time during peak hours when the system is operating closest to capacity. He also tries to measure his lead time, so he can make accurate promises to his customers. This includes internal customers, like John and Wink, as well as the external customers who are consuming his food. Lucky is also proactive about working with the dining room manager, John, who pitches in from time to time, to make the best use of the dining room's collective human resources.

The importance of lead time as a measurement and the management of lead time as a practice can be seen with Web-based retailers like Zappos, which offers free 2-day shipping (1 day for VIP customers) and free returns. Zappos' value proposition is that it offers a huge variety of products—primarily shoes and clothes—in all price ranges, with free shipping and free returns. The 2-day lead time for receiving purchased goods is integral to the virtual shopping experience, because the customer can easily exchange different sizes without waiting days or weeks between the receipt of various packages. Because exchanges and thus proper fit can be obtained more rapidly by the consumer, Zappos has a customer base that is more satisfied, more quickly. A short lead time—supported by additional inventory—is an integral part of the Zappos value proposition.

TRADE-OFFS

Operational decisions are evaluated across multiple dimensions. In the face of limited resources, not all of the dimensions can be optimized. Trade-offs must be made among the OWC—in other words, speed might need to be sacrificed for quality, or cost might need to be sacrificed for the ability to customize. An organization cannot be all things to all people.

The most obvious trade-off in the Walden-Aster is the one that Chloe and Jennifer need to make when ordering. Neither woman is in the mood for a salad, and both want a hot meal. They may wistfully examine the custom menu items, but in the end, each chooses the quicker option. All consumers make these trade-offs when making a purchase. This is another important element of the concept of OWC. Companies should be aware of the OWC that are part of their value proposition, because these are the same trade-offs that customers consider when making a purchase decision.

The staff at the Walden-Aster makes another important trade-off by allowing children in the dining room. The Walden-Aster's mission is to serve world-class food and provide superior customer service to all dining patrons. This means, for them, allowing toddlers in the dining room while preserving a peaceful setting for other diners—which takes some fancy footwork. Businesses must consider their target audiences, and make operating and policy decisions that achieve their business goals while preserving the integrity of their mission. The decision to serve or target an additional customer segment might negatively impact the service experience of a first, core segment. This might then affect total sales.

BRAIN PLAY

1. How do Lucky, Wink, and the rest of the staff of the Walden-Aster manage variability in customer orders? What are their strategies for managing capacity? How do they utilize lead time? What is the role of inventory? How do these strategies for the management of order variability correspond to the menu offerings?
2. How does a fast-food restaurant differ from the Walden-Aster in its approach to managing variability?
3. How do you take into account the trade-offs between inventory, lead time, and capacity in your personal and/or professional life? How is this similar to the management of the Walden-Aster dining room? How is it different?

CHAPTER 3

Understanding Little's Law

DYLAN AND AMELIA HAVE A CUPPA

Dylan Smith was a self-employed executive recruiter in Washington, DC. He maintained a small office with a staff of two near the White House. His clientele were mostly government agencies and security-related businesses and consultancies.

Because of the continually changing political environment on Capitol Hill, relationship management was an important part of his job. He spent a good deal of time schmoozing at various political events, which he enjoyed, but which made it difficult to be home for dinner with his wife and three daughters without significant attention to his schedule.

Dylan Smith and Amelia Cantor reconnect over coffee. They observe the customers waiting in line to order coffee and notice the dynamics of the two different coffee lines. Then, they analyze Dylan's executive placement service and draw parallels between the two.

As you read the story, think about the concept of *customer as inventory* and the process of managing the customer experience from end to end. Also, consider the circumstances that might allow two different shops with the same throughput rate to have different throughput times.

One bright morning in December, Dylan had an early coffee appointment with Amelia Cantor, an executive he'd placed 6 months prior. His goals were to follow up on her experience and to keep his ear to the ground on other openings in the field. She was the new director of a nongovernmental consultancy that ran public health projects in North

Africa. Due to the region's proximity to the Middle East, the position needed to be filled by someone with a unique combination of qualifications, which she had.

Some days have this perfect flow of energy right from the start, he mused as he edged his car into a perfectly sized space right outside a new coffee place, Theron's Better Cup. He was surprised to see through the window that the line was not as long as he expected.

On entering, he observed two lines: a longer, faster line in front of two large thermal carafes of coffee, and a shorter, slower line in front of an array of individual coffee drip stands. He got in the longer of the two lines and was handed two large, steaming cups of freshly brewed perfection in under 2 minutes. He found a table for two near a window. *Perfect*, he thought.

He claimed the table with his coat and one of the coffees, then headed over to a condiment table to add his requisite sugar and cream. He counted no fewer than four condiment tables spaced throughout the shop. Although some stock-out was unavoidable, a customer who suddenly found him- or herself without sufficient half-and-half could check the supply at another table.

As a result of all this, the coffee shop was able to accommodate quite a number of paying customers, each happily engaged in conversation or nose-deep in a laptop. Amelia's arrival snapped Dylan out of his reverie, and he waved her over.

Amelia: Have you been here before?

Dylan: No, I haven't. I'm impressed with their efficiency! I can't believe how many tables they've crammed into this little place, or how good they are at filling orders.

Amelia: I've been here with my kids. They serve a whole line of premade food as well, which bumps up their cash receipts per customer. My kids like the yogurt parfaits, and that game area over there is just their speed, so I can let them play after they're done eating, and I can have a conversation with a friend or check my e-mail.

Dylan: Their biggest expense is probably the rent.

Amelia: Oh, by far. This is Capitol Hill, after all. And an independent coffee shop doesn't have the buying power that a large chain does. I think the reason they survive is that they're so good at filling orders and have so many places to sit. Even though it's crammed, you can easily get your condiments and find a seat. They keep the turnover high.

Dylan: So what do you think is their secret?

Amelia: Well, it's the throughput rate combined with the average receipt per customer, right? I think it all comes down to pipeline management. We have pipelines, too, but we have different considerations.

Dylan: I'm not sure I understand. Doesn't pipeline management imply some sort of inventory? The coffee?

Amelia: Actually, here, the people waiting in line are the inventory. It's a customer pipeline. The pipeline in this case would be the set of activities that begins the moment a person enters the building and ends the moment he or she sits at a table. The completion of all those activities takes place in a certain time frame—from the customer's point of view—and the customers keep coming at a certain frequency or rate—from the barista's point of view. So however long it takes one person to go through the whole set of steps is the *throughput time*, and the number of people who enter the system in a given time frame is the *throughput rate*. Multiply those two things, and you have your inventory.

If it takes everybody the same amount of time, but more people get in line, the line will get longer. If the flow of people entering the shop holds steady, but each person takes longer and longer to add cream and sugar, the number of people in the store will increase.

Dylan: But if people take longer in line, doesn't that mean that fewer people get through?

Amelia: No. You're confusing throughput rate and throughput time. Let's say the average time in line is 3 minutes, and 60 people arrive per hour. If 60 people arrive in an hour, one arrives every minute. The average line length would be three people. If you could reduce the time in line to 2 minutes, the line length would go down to two people, but you would still get 60 people per hour. Similarly, if the time in the line increased to 4 minutes, the line length would go up, but you could still get 60 people through the shop in an hour.

Dylan: Also, why did you end the pipeline when the customer sits down at the table? Doesn't it matter how long the tables are in use? Why don't you measure the amount of time between when a customer enters the door and when he or she exits the building?

Amelia: You actually can, if you want. It's all a matter of where you "draw the box." In this kind of place, not everybody sits down. Some leave.

Dylan: Well, why not just measure how long it takes for one customer to wait in line?

Amelia: You could, but then you wouldn't be considering other factors, like how long it takes to add condiments and find a table. These things factor directly into customer satisfaction. Until you're sitting down, enjoying your beverage, your order hasn't really been filled, has it?

Actually, if you want to get really comprehensive, then you should take into account the average length of time it takes to find a parking spot—a legal one—and walk to the building. This is technically part of the time it takes for a potential customer to make a decision about patronizing the establishment and being satisfied that his or her investment of time and money has been rewarded.

Ease of getting to this coffee shop is a big part of it, too. That's why they're willing to pay the high rent. They wouldn't have nearly the traffic that they do if they hadn't considered the shared merchant parking lot behind the block or the increase in foot traffic that they enjoy from being so close to the Metro stop. I'd venture to say that their customer pipeline actually begins the moment that someone thinks about their coffee—wherever he or she is geographically—and ends the moment he or she sits down with a hot cup. If it's too difficult to get here and the potential customer decides to go somewhere else instead, that sale is lost—there's leakage in the system—and that's part of the model.

But I'm not sure that the cycle ends when the customer walks out the door, even though that's part of the experience that they pay for—and expect—when they spend money here. I'm just not sure it's part of the order fulfillment process. But I could be convinced otherwise.

Dylan: I see exactly what you're saying about applying this line of thinking to my own business model.

Amelia: Well, yes. You work for yourself. Defining a metric that you can use to keep track of your customer pipeline inventory should be something you use to measure your effectiveness and efficiency. So how would you define your customer pipeline parameters?

Dylan: Well, I have two kinds of inventory, organizations and candidates, and I need both—I'm essentially a matchmaker. The customer conversion process begins with either a direct referral or a visit to my website. Whoever it is will look at my website before contacting me. So my Internet storefront is really important, because it's the first thing people will see. My value proposition and credibility are imperative. It's essential to communicate my track record, credentials, and confidentiality right up front, especially because the industry I serve most often is connected with homeland security.

Amelia: Yes, I can see that. And your website does communicate those things—mostly because you have a terrific reputation. So what's next?

Dylan: Well, if the prospective is a candidate, then he or she will send me a résumé, and I'll assess the candidate—background checks, references, all that. So that process is part of the candidate pipeline. Then, I might have to give it some time before the right opportunity presents itself. Sometimes there's an immediate match, and sometimes there's not. So the number of clients I have in my other customer pipeline—the organizations—directly affects the candidate pipeline. I can't take someone out of the first one until they can enter the second!

Amelia: That makes sense, yes. What are the parameters for the client, or "target company," pipeline?

Dylan: The companies don't always have a vacancy that needs filling when they initially find out about me. If I keep in touch with the potential client and continue to remind them of my abilities, then they're more likely to hire me when they have a need. The length of time it takes me to convert a potential client to a paying customer depends on how well I maintain contact and keep up my value proposition, which is simple: I can fill your positions with the greatest rate of success because I'm trustworthy and have access to the highest qualified, most vetted candidates in the industry. And I'd say my pipelines converge when a match is made and I get a check in the mail. Both pipelines have to be as short as possible. I don't want to keep placements waiting, and I don't want to keep target companies waiting.

Not only is it a part of the service, but I don't convert either of them into cash until they've both made it through.

Some businesses have more of a linear pipeline, like the one we're sitting in now, but my combined pipelines become shorter when my selection is greater. That is, it's easier for me to make the best match when I have more candidates and more target companies to choose from. So the average time spent in the pipeline for each candidate becomes shorter when I have access to more people. The likelihood of identifying a qualified match increases.

Amelia: That makes sense when you think about it in those terms. Have you thought about using metrics to describe the ways in which your two pipelines interact? Because they're obviously dependent on one another, even though they're defined by two distinct sets of events.

Dylan: No, I haven't, but I'll give it some thought. Meanwhile, I'm glad they don't kick you out of the coffee shop after you've been sitting at one of their tables for a half an hour, because that's about how long we've been here. Look at the time!

Amelia: Well, let's get down to business, then! I'll tell you all about the job. You can use it as a testimonial on your website!

MOVING CUSTOMERS
THROUGH A PIPELINE

LITTLE'S LAW

Little's Law says that a customer's time spent in line is a product of the number of people in line and the average time spent serving each person. For example, a line with an average of three people, each taking an average of 15 minutes to serve, would be longer to wait in than a line that contains an average of 15 people, each taking an average of 2 minutes

Lean Takeaways

Almost all the benefits of Lean can be explained through Little's Law. The goal of Lean is to reduce cycle time or the cash-conversion cycle. By reducing the time required to convert prospective candidates into placements, Dylan can increase his working capital and free it up for other endeavors. The coffee shop benefits from applying Little's Law, as well—because it is more profitable when waiting times are short and customers are satisfied.

The next story is the last in the "Customer" section and extends our Little's Law thinking to an understanding of a concept called "single-piece flow."

to serve. This is technically an equation—which we said we wouldn't give you—but it's so central to operations and Lean that we thought we'd include it as an important *relationship* rather than something that needs to be solved numerically. Using our example above:

Line 1: 3 people × 15 minutes = 45 minutes to get through the line on average.
Line 2: 15 people × 2 minutes = 30 minutes to get through the line on average.

Line 1 has a *throughput time* (TPT) of 45 minutes (0.75 hours).
Line 2 has a TPT of 30 minutes (0.5 hours).

Line 1 has a *throughput rate* (TPR) of one person every 15 minutes, or four per hour.
Line 2 has a TPR of one person every 2 minutes, or 30 per hour.

The number of people in line at any given time (the "inventory") can be calculated by multiplying TPT by TPR. This just means that if you know how long people are waiting in line (TPT) and you can create a fraction that expresses that one person is served per some average amount of time (TPR), then you can multiply these to figure out the average number of people in line. Using the same example:

Line 1: # people (Inventory) = 0.75 hours (TPT) × 4 (TPR) = 3 people in line
Line 2: # people (Inventory) = 0.5 hours (TPT) × 30 (TPR) = 15 people in line

Little's Law explains systems where the average TPR is less than the capability of the system to accommodate demand. On average, a line is like an accordion. It can expand and contract randomly over time. As long as the average number of people entering a system is less than the capacity of the system to fill orders, then TPR is defined by the rate of demand. Once more people enter the line on average than can be served by the barista, then the barista becomes a bottleneck and the line begins to build up. At this time, the TPR of the system is no longer equal to demand (i.e., the number of customers entering the line) but becomes the capacity of the bottleneck process (i.e., the barista can serve only one customer every 4 minutes). If no more baristas are added at peak demand times to add capacity to the system, then TPR is limited by the barista's speed, and the line will continue to grow until demand slows down again.

Little's Law can help us understand the two different lines for coffee in Theron's Better Cup, the coffee shop we talked about in the first chapter. The first line is longer and quicker because coffee is premade and dispensed from thermal carafes. The second line likely has fewer people in it but takes longer, because custom-made coffee is ground and drip-brewed separately for each customer.

Little's Law is useful as a broad-brush, back-of-the-napkin approach to measuring the order-filling capacity of any given system. How many new customer "orders" enter a system in a given period of time, and how long does it take to fill each order? The total number in the pipeline is equal to the first quantity multiplied by the second. "How long will it take for my meal to arrive?" asks a patron at a restaurant who has just placed the order. "Well, that depends on the number of orders already waiting and the length of time each order takes to fill" would be an accurate reply. Of course, many factors are contained within each of these two measurements, but Little's Law is a good place to start improving delivery of the value promised to customers.

PIPELINE MANAGEMENT

Amelia defines the coffee shop's *customer pipeline* as beginning the moment that a potential customer thinks about coffee and ending the moment they leave the establishment. For the purposes of simplicity, she shortens the pipeline so that it begins when the customer walks in the door and ends when he or she sits down at a table with their coffee. Amelia and Dylan discuss the choices that affect the TPR or TPT of the system from end to end, since TPT multiplied by TPR (see the example in the "Little's Law" section of this chapter) yields the average number of customers in the pipeline. In this pipeline, the customers are the inventory.

What insights can we gain from Amelia and Dylan's conversation in the coffee shop that can help us understand the following:

- Little's Law?
- Pipeline management?
- The cash conversion cycle?

The two-line design affects total average time in line. One line is faster but has only two options, and the other is slower and has many options. Customers can choose whether they want a quicker cup or a more customized cup. Customers can move through the pipeline at different TPTs depending on what kind of coffee they want. The length of the line will depend on the number of people who select each line.

TPT is decreased at Theron's Better Cup because customers can customize coffee at self-serve cream-and-sugar counters, and because there are a large number of available tables. The total time spent in line is reduced because customers do not spend time adding their condiments until later. The capacity of the bottleneck resource—the baristas' time—is not wasted on activities the customers can perform themselves. Customers can also easily find a place to sit after obtaining and customizing their coffee.

The total number of people in the coffee shop is increased because the coffee shop is located in a dense, downtown area with high foot traffic. It's crowded. The number of people coming into the coffee shop is the TPR (demand). As the number of customers increases during times of peak demand and the coffee shop gets closer to capacity (i.e., the bottleneck), then both the line length and the total waiting time will increase. The "inventory" of the customer pipeline, which in this case begins when the customer enters the shop and ends when he or she leaves, is the customers. In order to move customers through the pipeline more quickly during times of peak demand, thus reducing "inventory" (i.e., crowding), management would need to identify the bottleneck and increase its capacity. In this case, the bottleneck might be barista time, or it might be the number of tables.

There are some pipelines for which a greater TPR decreases TPT. For example, Dylan also maintains two pipelines, one for job candidates and one for jobs. When he has a greater variety or quantity of candidates and jobs, his TPR might be higher (more successful matches per week), and his TPT might be lower (candidates and employers spend less time looking) because, with more options to choose from, he is more likely to find a good match and obtain satisfied customers.

The customer's experience while in the pipeline should be matched to the value proposition—in other words, the benefits for which customers are willing to pay (OWC). Amelia looks at Theron's Better Cup as a holistic customer experience when she mentions that the true coffee pipeline begins the moment when the customer thinks about the coffee and ends when they leave the establishment. Choices such as ease of finding the location and sufficient available parking are all part of the customer's experience. Broadly, all operation design choices that affect the pipeline conditions and the customer experience should closely relate to and reflect the value proposition.

CASH CONVERSION CYCLE

The cash conversion cycle is a measurement of time between when inputs to a process are purchased (raw materials, labor, overhead, etc.) and when money is received after a sale. Through Lean thinking, the cash conversion cycle can be reduced. A just-in-time manufacturing approach limits inventory in a system. Limited inventory can lower TPT while maintaining the same TPR as a high-inventory system. By decreasing the amount of work-in-process inventory in the system, two things happen. First, the amount of capital tied up in a nonproductive asset is reduced (net working capital). Second, lead time is reduced, and customer orders can be filled more quickly and with more flexibility.

This is explained by Little's Law. Two processes can have the same TPR (demand) yet shorter or longer pipelines. The process with the shorter pipeline, which has less inventory, yields a lower investment and shorter lead times. This creates value for both the customer and the company.

BRAIN PLAY

1. What metrics could Dylan use to numerically describe the behavior of his two pipelines: buyers and sellers?
2. How could a bank use Little's Law to calculate pipelines of days receivable and days payable?
3. Think about a situation in your personal or professional life where you could apply Little's Law. What insights can you gain from its use?

CHAPTER 4

Achieving Single-Piece Flow

BELINDA, BAGS, AND BATCHES

Around 2:00 p.m. on Thanksgiving Day, as guests began to arrive, Belinda Daniel took the turkey, glistening and brown, out of the oven. She had left just enough time to whip up some gravy on the stovetop and warm up the mashed potatoes and sweet potato casserole that had been cooked the day before.

As her friends and family entertained themselves and waited for mealtime, Belinda peered into cabinets that had not been cleaned out in over a year and failed to find any flour for the gravy. All the activity was starting to give her a headache, so she took some ibuprofen.

Belinda Daniel takes a break from her Thanksgiving preparations and her houseguests to pop out to the grocery store for a few last-minute items. While checking out at the self-checkout line, she thinks about different designs for checkout lines and their effect on customer wait times. She considers how to determine the quantity that should be processed at the same time.

As you read Belinda's story, think about the different reasons that might exist for identifying an optimal batch size, and the relationship between batch size and wait time. What do stores consider when designing checkout lines?

"I need to go to the store," she announced to no one in particular. "I'll be right back."

At the grocery store, many other people were taking short breaks from their cooking duties to pick up last-minute items. Belinda grabbed a basket, found the flour and some detergent, and pondered whether to' use one of the traditional grocery store lines or a self-serve express lane. She wasn't in a hurry to return to her kitchen, but the store was warm and noisy, and she wanted to get back outside to the cooler air to help her headache.

The lines were longer at the self-serve stations, but each customer had only one or two items. Although the full-service lines were shorter, the customers in them had carts that were full to overflowing. Belinda went with a line for one of the six self-checkouts.

MT '11

While Belinda waited, she watched a few of the full-service lines to see if people in those lines got through before she did. One line lacked a bagger, so checked cans and cartons slid up against bread and lettuce. At another line, an elderly man squinted at the total above the cash register and then began writing in his checkbook, at the same time chatting with the clerk. She could see the light flashing at another cash register, indicating the need for a price check. Meanwhile, six people ahead of her in her self-checkout line had finished with the process.

As Belinda had watched her line and the other self-checkout lines, she had seen delays from time to time as customers had trouble entering their frequent-shopper numbers or finding the barcodes on items. A store employee helped customers get through the self-checkout stations. Belinda felt that she had chosen the right service line.

She had also been watching the store's bagging system. At other stores, self-serve checkout stations used a half-length conveyor belt system; customers scanned their items and then placed them on the belt. Scanned items moved along the belt, where they stayed until the customer paid for them and then placed them in bags.

In this particular store, the bags were arranged on a stand, so that as one bag filled up, the patron could easily start to fill another one, and a customer only had to pick up the item, scan it, and place it directly in the bag. Belinda remembered that the belt system in the other store took more time, since it required a customer to pick up an item, place it on the belt, and then pick it up a second time to place it in a bag after payment. In addition, to avoid confusion, the next customer had to wait while the customer ahead bagged groceries.

Finally, it was her turn, and she paid for her items and left: one bag in each hand, the load divided between the right and the left. As she walked, she reflected on the difference between the two bagging systems, one that processed items in batches and one that processed each item completely, one at a time.

"It all depends on context," she thought. "I'm not going to feed each guest one at a time, wash their dishes, then move on to the next one. The size of a batch, and the parts of a process included in that batch, have to make sense for the process as a whole.

"Everything we do all day long is divided into batches. Our laundry is done in batches—sometimes lights and darks, and sometimes just thrown in together because we are in a hurry. And then there's the food that we eat. How many of our calories for the day do we eat at one sitting? Different cultures divide their calories into different numbers of meals. But sometimes it's more effective to process single items all the way through, then start all over with another item—and not only big items that make more sense to process one at a time. By picking up each grocery item only once, I reduced my personal energy and effort requirements by 50%. What about all the paper and mail that accumulate at home? When I make piles of these things, they require more sorting, which means more handling. Maybe batches don't make sense with things that can be processed immediately but need to be dealt with one at a time. If I put the whole stack of mail on my desk, then I might miss an important bill, but if I go through each piece immediately and make a decision about it, not only will I reduce the chance of missing something important, but I will also reduce clutter and use less energy.

"How often do I buy clothes for the kids or for myself? Do I wait until everything I own is faded or out of style and then spend a huge sum replacing everything? Or do I go shopping more often for fewer items as they become worn or some other need arises? I tend to do the latter because it evens out the money I spend monthly maintaining my wardrobe. My children grow out of their clothes within a season. I often receive bags of slightly used clothes from other mothers whose children are older than my own. So batch processing still makes sense for them, where it might not for me. A bag of clothes is their batch!

"The context is what makes the difference."

Belinda entered the house with her bags. Her headache was gone.

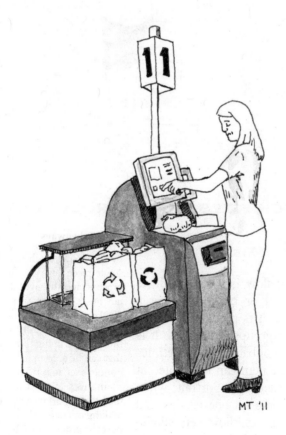

MT '11

BATCH SIZES AT THE GROCERY STORE

SINGLE-PIECE FLOW

Single-piece flow is when products are generated or created one at a time, even if it is possible to create products in groups or batches. It is the opposite of batching. Sometimes only a single item can be created at one time, such as a portrait, when an artist works on one canvas at a time. Sometimes, however, single-piece flow is a choice that is made even when there are other options.

Lean Takeaways

By decreasing batch size and achieving single-piece flow, working capital, work in process, and throughput time can be simultaneously reduced—a primary component of a Lean implementation. Another method for reducing inventory and throughput time is identifying those setup activities that can be accomplished offline (single-minute exchange of die, or SMED).

In this section, "Customer," we examined the importance of identifying and making operation design choices that support the order-winning criteria. The next section, "Capability," focuses on operational decisions that deliver the value proposition.

Belinda observes the checkout line of a grocery store when she is in a rush but the lines are long. Belinda compares two different types of self-checkout registers at grocery stores. The first requires the customer to scan all the items (a batch) before then bagging all the items (also a batch). The second checkout line allows the user to immediately bag his or her purchases using a carousel-style bag holder. In this context, the ability to scan the item and place it in the bag with one motion (single-piece flow) is preferable to the batch system. Batching at the checkout counter forces the customer to scan all the items and then handle each item again while bagging it. The items are handled twice instead of once, and the line takes longer overall because each user's time at the station is increased. Subsequent customers can't use the scanner until the current customer finishes bagging, creating further delay. Throughput time (TPT) is increased and throughput rate (TPR) is decreased—rarely a good combination!

THE SOCIAL CONTRACT AND PERCEPTIONS OF FAIRNESS

The challenge for any queue-based operation is to maintain transparency and realistic expectations. Customers should feel as if their needs are being addressed in good faith and that they are being dealt with fairly. Otherwise, passing or being passed in line, for example, can be viewed as a betrayal of that faith and a travesty of justice that can quickly result in loss of business and negative publicity.

Belinda makes judgments about her experience based on her perceptions of fairness. She looks at other grocery store patrons in the lines next to her to see who reaches the front of the line first. She notes that her 12-person line is nearly six down, while next to her, a full-service line is paused because a blinking "I need help from a manager" light is on. She doesn't think much of this, because she thinks the self-service lines and full-service lines are different in terms of their promised value or experience to customers. Second, she notes that an older gentleman who enjoys his personal interactions with the checker is taking longer than he otherwise could, while those behind him wait. She also doesn't place a negative value judgment on this, because she has some tolerance for the intangible social needs of people (i.e., the human element) in any process.

STANDARD WORK AND VARIABILITY

Standard work is the idea that every step in a process should be defined and performed in the same way each time. Work is standardized in an effort to reduce variability, because variability can produce defects or increase risk. Standard work is also the documentation of best practices in the current state of a process. As a system is improved, over time, a "new normal" results, and the description of best practices should be updated. Standard work is as follows:

- The precise work sequence through which an operator performs work tasks within a specified time.
- The standard inventory, including units in machines, required to keep the process running smoothly.[1]

Standard work reduces variability. Taking note of the causes of variability can help to reduce it and make it possible to define standard work. Belinda notices that the following events prevent the line from running smoothly:

- A bagger is not available in a full-service line.
- Customers have trouble locating frequent-shopper numbers.
- Unusually shaped objects may not scan well, either by a checker or by the inexperienced self-checker.
- Younger patrons are asked to show identification to purchase alcohol.
- Customers take out checkbooks *after* their food has been rung up, instead of preparing the check while the groceries are being scanned.

Identifying and reducing events that might contribute to delaying a process would be one way of reaching a "new normal" in terms of the standard work of a process.

Businesses define standard work when they first begin a process improvement journey. The current- and future-state vision is a starting point to begin broad, strategic, leadership-point-of-view decisions about where an organization or process is and where it should be. The

---

[1] Lean Enterprise Institute, "Standardized Work: The Foundation for Kaizen," retrieved November 26, 2011, from http://www.lean.org/workshops/WorkshopDescription. cfm?WorkshopId=20

standard work analysis provides a closer look at the process as it exists today, so that meaningful improvement steps can occur.

SMED (SETUP TIME REDUCTION)

What does Belinda think about at the store that can help us understand the following:

- Optimal batch size?
- Single-piece flow?
- Critical path?
- Single-minute exchange of die (SMED)?
- The social contract and perceptions of fairness?
- Standard work and variability?

The phrase *single-minute exchange of die* (SMED) originated in the Japanese manufacturing industry. SMED refers to setup time reduction as a form of process improvement. First, activities are identified that can be performed during a machine's running time (uptime), and others are identified that can be done *only* while the machine is off (downtime). As many tasks as possible should be performed while the machine is running, and tasks that can *only* be performed during the downtime of the machine should be consolidated, minimized, and streamlined. This allows the amount of time spent on machine setup to be reduced and maximizes the running time of a machine—thereby increasing capacity and productive time.

When a man that Belinda observes in a full-service grocery line takes out his checkbook and starts to fill it out *after* his groceries have been rung up, he delays the progress of the line. The "machine" in this case is the checker ringing up his groceries. The man could have taken out his checkbook while the groceries were being rung up (machine uptime) and begun to fill it out—and left only the last step, filling in the amount due on the check, to perform after the groceries had passed into the bagging area (machine downtime). If he had done so, he would have taken advantage of the machine's uptime to prepare the check. His total checkout time would have been shorter, and he would not have delayed the line for others.

In addition to manufacturing examples, there are many everyday situations that reveal the benefits of setup reduction.[2] In the past, recorded popular music was produced and consumed in song "batches" in the

---

[2] These examples are sourced from Rebecca Goldberg and Elliott Weiss, *Lean Thinking: Better Living through Setup Reduction* (Charlottesville, VA: Darden Business Publishing, 2013).

form of LP albums, cassette tapes, or compact discs. A customer's setup time consisted of traveling to a music store, sorting through the inventory, and selecting an item to purchase. When an online order is placed for a single song and the order is filled instantly via downloading or streaming, the setup time required to produce the order is virtually zero. A digital product eliminates the need for setup.

Print media have also shown significant setup time reduction along with batch size reduction. Previously, news articles were "batched" together in the form of weekly or daily newspapers. The setup time for these batches included editorial, layout, printing, and distribution via bicycle, street vendor, or corner store. Cloud-based reporting now offers the possibility of a batch size of one tweet or one article. Delivery time is instantaneous, and there is no setup time for an order once the digital layout is complete.

In new product development, rapid-cycle experimentation is an illustration of SMED-like thinking. Consider testing 10 features of a new product under development. You can batch these tests prior to release by performing them all at once, or you can conduct the experiments one at a time in a sequence. The shorter cycle of testing and feedback can limit exposure to risk and loss by identifying and implementing improvements quickly, especially if the features are independent of each other. Another option is that if only the first five improvements are critical, the remaining five could be conducted after release. Any choice to perform actions all at once or in sequence is related to SMED-like thinking about batch size and setup time.

Any golfer who prepares for the next shot while their playing partner is taking his or her shot is practicing SMED-like thinking by taking activities offline. Casino patrons also experience the benefits of setup reduction. Many blackjack tables now employ automatic card shufflers. Once a hand is played, cards are placed into a continuous shuffling machine, eliminating the need for the dealer to shuffle the cards between hands. This increases the number of rounds of blackjack that can be played in a given time period. Poker tables employ two decks of cards; as one deck is played, the second deck is shuffled offline, yielding the same benefit. At Disney World, some attractions use the Omnimover system, a type of conveyer system that runs continuously, eliminating any setup time associated with unloading and loading riders.

BRAIN PLAY

1. What batching opportunities does Belinda have? What are the trade-offs involved in these decisions?
2. What might the benefits of single-piece flow be for a pharmaceutical manufacturer? What might the benefits and challenges be in implementing such a system?
3. Think about a situation in your personal or professional life for which a different batch size or single-piece flow might be more appropriate. What might be the barriers to making these changes?

PART II

Capability

CHAPTER 5

Managing Constrained Resources

DONNA JOHNSON
AND THE BOTTLENECKS

Donna Johnson's jewelry design orders skyrocket overnight after a local wedding magazine features her work. While researching ways to scale up to meet the increased demand, she realizes that she is the bottleneck. Donna encounters a second bottleneck in her apartment's shared laundry room, where someone has left wet clothes in the dryer without turning it on.

As you read Donna's story, think about how she manages her bottlenecks and what factors she considers when making decisions.

Donna Johnson lived in Trendy Hills, an apartment complex just north of the graduate business school where her husband, Jordan, was a first-year MBA student. Donna had given birth to their son, Jake, only months before Jordan entered the program, and because her husband was often gone until late at night, Donna frequently found herself alone in the apartment with the baby. Out of boredom one day, she began to read the large casebooks that Jordan kept stacked in a precarious pile by the front door. Her favorites were the cases on operations.

Donna decided that she would do something with her time, so she began to research ideas for small businesses. She knew she'd stumbled upon something great when she saw some advertisements on Facebook for a local jewelry maker. "My designs are more stylish than that," she thought. "I could drive traffic to a website with my own jewelry, using social media and other search engine optimization techniques. It's the perfect way to spend the time that Jake doesn't need me."

She started small, with a line of 10 designs, each requiring an average of $15 worth of materials and 20 minutes of assembly time. She priced them at $45, which she figured would net her $90 an hour for the time she spent making them. The time she spent on marketing matched her time in production, so if she averaged the money made over the total time spent, it yielded an hourly rate of almost $45. Additionally, she had some startup costs: investment in cut-glass beads and sterling silver clasps; hooks and chains; website photography and creation; and her single Facebook ad, which cost a whopping $350. Altogether, the startup cost was close to $1,500. She figured she'd replenish her material inventory at a rate that matched production and sales, so she would always maintain approximately the same level of stock with which she began.

It was a perfect setup. After a slow start out of the gate, her designs caught on quickly. Three months after her website launch, an article was written about her in the local paper's wedding section, highlighting the beautiful wedding necklace that was part of the collection. The article also featured some of her other designs on bridesmaids, in various colors. Overnight, she was a celebrity!

Initially, this was good news for the Johnson family. They were able to pay off some credit card debt and begin a college savings plan for Jake. Then, one evening, Jordan arrived home after midnight to find his wife asleep, sprawled atop a mound of cut-glass beads, drooling out of the corner of her mouth into a bowl of turquoise pendants. He managed to rouse her.

Jordan: Honey, I'm worried about you. What's going on?

Donna: Oh, it's these jewelry orders. I can't fill them all. There isn't enough of me to go around these days.

Jordan: But you're so successful! Everyone is talking about you at school. I'm the most popular guy in the first-year program because of you.

Donna: That's great, sweetie, but what's going to happen next week if I can't get all these bridal adornments out on time? If it starts getting out that I ruined three weddings because I couldn't get to the post office on time, that'll be the end of it.

Jordan: Maybe you need to take a break. We don't need the money that badly.

Donna: Maybe there's another way. Maybe I should outsource my operation to India.

Jordan: Um, honey, you have a home business making jewelry.

Donna: So? I read your operations casebook and technical notes. I am the bottleneck. And my business will accommodate the increased throughput rate if I can eliminate it. I just have to replace myself, preferably with two or three of me, and pay these new versions of myself less!

Jordan: Okay, sounds great. Can I help?

Donna: You just go ahead and finish that MBA. I'll take care of "bid-ness" here at the ranch.

Jordan: Okay, well, now that my wife has completely left the building, can we go to sleep?

Donna: You can. I need to finish Mindy's bridesmaid's rosettes. I'll see you in the morning. [*Baby cries.*] On second thought, you can get Jake for me. I guess we should feed him.

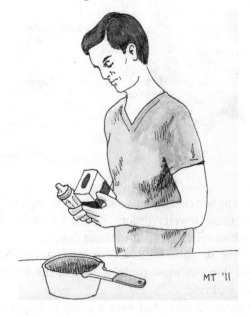

The next day, while Jake was down for his morning nap, Donna did some research on outsourcing. She learned she could hire some high school students to put together her designs for $10 an hour.

Donna then turned her attention to the laundry, which she had been hiding behind the bedroom door. She moved the door, and at least four loads' worth fell to her feet.

Donna scooped up all the laundry into a large sheet, strapped Jake into a front carrier, and maneuvered this entire arrangement down two flights of steps into the laundry room. She loaded about half the laundry into the available washers, leaving the rest on the floor. She began talking to Jake.

Donna: What a mess. And you know what, Jake? We have to stay down here for hours now. There are two washing machines that take 30 minutes to run through a cycle. There are also two dryers—but they take an hour! So if we stay down here for the first half hour, we can switch the laundry and get our second two loads running. What do you say?

Jake was more focused on gumming the carrier, so the two wandered around outside and returned as the washer cycle was ending. Donna opened the dryer to find someone else's wet clothes.

Donna: Gross. Jake, this is just gross. What do I do with these wet clothes? I mean, I have to take them out, right? When do I get to dry my clothes? The washing machine just finished, and my stuff can't sit there molding for half an hour. I need them to be dried now!

[David, another apartment resident, entered the shared facility.]

David: Oh, sorry. I must have forgotten to start the load. Are you guys having a good day?

Donna: Fabulous. I'll come back in a bit. This laundry room is such a bottleneck! If they had twice as many dryers as washers, you could wash and dry clothes all day long at the same rate, and you'd never back up into the guy in front of you, right?

David: That assumes everybody remembers to turn the dryer on.

MANAGING THE LIMITED RESOURCES OF TIME, CAPACITY, AND MONEY

BOTTLENECKS

A bottleneck is the slowest process in a set of processes or *system*. The system can be linear (in a line, one at a time), cyclical (in a circle), or parallel (two or more at a time). One effect of a bottleneck is that it sets the pace, or through-put rate (TPR), for the entire system. We learned about the TPR in Section 1, Chapter 3, "Dylan and Amelia Have a Cuppa." For example, if a dough-nut must pass through four machines before reaching the end of a production line, and the third machine can process

Lean Takeaways

When scaling up a business process, the primary task is to identify and reduce the impact of bottlenecks on the productivity of the process. Decreasing cost, increasing qual-ity, and improving delivery are all effectiveness measures that can be affected by an unaddressed bottleneck. Bottlenecks can occur at any point in a process, and they can be related to labor, capital, or natural resources.

This section, "Capability," focuses on the delivery of the value proposi-tion through process excellence. The next several chapters will examine process improvement activities for delivering customer value.

40 doughnuts per minute while the other machines can process 60 doughnuts per minute, the entire system must still operate at no more than 40 doughnuts per minute.

Another effect of a bottleneck is that the rest of the system is never fully utilized. The bottleneck process is most likely always running, since everything else is dependent on what the bottleneck produces. The non-bottleneck processes are idle while they are waiting. Idle time is not necessarily a bad thing, because the waiting time may prevent unnecessary inventory from building up—and managing the extra inventory would require additional resources.

Donna Johnson experiences the negative effects of her bottleneck (time) because she cannot fill all her orders. Her health suffers as a result of working near her capacity. She attempts to do what many managers do when they recognize a bottleneck—run the machine with the bottleneck near (or over!) its capacity in an effort to speed up the entire system. This approach, however, whether in the context of people or machines, often results in problems relating to overwork. Donna's husband, Jordan, notices that his wife is suffering and helps her look for a solution.

The ratio of washing machines to clothes dryers in Donna's laundry room is another example of a bottleneck. Since the washers run a 30-minute cycle and the dryers run a 60-minute cycle, laundry would flow smoothly through the laundry room only if there were twice as many dryers as washers. If there were twice as many dryers as washers, all the machines could run at once and no wet laundry would sit for half an hour while waiting for a dryer to free up. Another unique aspect of the bottleneck in the laundry room—as opposed to the bottleneck in Donna's jewelry production system—is that it is largely beyond Donna's control. The equipment and laundry room do not belong to her, and she is dependent on the goodwill and follow-through of the other apartment residents to keep laundry moving. In the business world as well, a person who is being affected by a bottleneck will be able to control some situations and not others. For example, a bottleneck might be in a support area out of an individual's direct control such as legal or accounting.

Typically, once a bottleneck is removed, another will present itself. This is because it is extremely unusual to find a perfectly matched set of processes. There will almost always be one process in a system that is slower than the rest. Management decisions about whether or not to invest in reducing a bottleneck should involve a comparison of cost and benefit. If resources are *not* spent trying to reduce the bottleneck, there are still costs related to keeping the system the way it is, including lost potential production, increased cost per unit, and the cost of maintaining the idle time of non-bottleneck machines. While there is a higher upfront cost when resources *are* spent trying to reduce a bottleneck, there are also benefits to improving the bottleneck—including the ability to produce more units and to produce them faster, and the increased capacity of the whole system.

Donna has chosen to increase the capacity of the bottleneck in her jewelry business—her time. This is called *elevating* the bottleneck. She does this by hiring additional workers. Donna might also want to do what is called *exploiting* the bottleneck by changing the way she makes her jewelry. She can reduce the amount of time she spends on each piece of jewelry by eliminating any non–value-added activities that currently use her time.

THEORY OF CONSTRAINTS

In 1977, Eliyahu M. Goldratt, an Israeli physicist-turned-management-consultant and philosopher, published *The Goal*, a novel about manufacturing. Goldratt illustrates that the goal of manufacturing organizations is to make money and that the process can be evaluated in terms of three criteria:

1. Throughput: the rate at which money is generated through sales
2. Inventory: the money invested in purchasing things intended for sale
3. Operating expense

The philosophy had three major tenets. First, scheduling to maximize production profitability must focus on constraints (bottlenecks) and match operational output to market demand. Second, he did not believe that use of the accounting technique called *standard costing* was useful.[1] Finally, Goldratt stressed that maximizing the efficiency of each single operation in a production process was quite often detrimental to the performance of the entire process.

---

[1] Standard costing is an accounting method that often does not accurately describe the true costs of each item produced. Instead, it uses averages and categories to assign a standard cost to each item.

Goldratt uses the metaphor of a troop of Boy Scouts hiking. The slowest scout (i.e., the bottleneck) is named Herbie. Today, if you go to manufacturing facilities in most parts of the world and ask, "Where's your Herbie?" the plant personnel will take you directly to their bottleneck machines. Donna is the "Herbie" in her jewelry business and the clothes dryer is the "Herbie" in the laundry room, because these two stages were the slowest.

Goldratt developed the Theory of Constraints (TOC) so he could generalize these concepts to other settings. TOC is a five-step process:

1. Identify the system's constraint(s).
2. Decide how to exploit the system's constraint(s).
3. Subordinate everything else to the decisions made in step 2.
4. Elevate the system's constraint(s).
5. If a constraint is broken in step 4, go back to step 1, but don't allow inertia to become the system's primary constraint.

Constraints (bottlenecks) should not limit the profitability or output of an organization. Once the constraint is identified, it should be "exploited." In TOC, exploitation means that management's attention should be focused on the constraint above all else. Because the bottleneck limits output, it should not be permitted to be idle. According to step 4 above, an hour lost at the bottleneck is an hour lost for the total system. In many organizations, the constraint may actually be sales or a lack of customers. Step 3 warns us not to let non-bottlenecks create constraints, and step 4 advises us to increase capacity at the bottleneck. Note that steps 2 and 3, through better system management, allow us to find hidden system capacity.

What can Donna's experiences with growing her jewelry business and doing her laundry help us understand more about:

- Bottlenecks?
- The Theory of Constraints?
- Scale-up?

SCALE-UP

Issues of scale-up are part of every startup's stories of "the days in the trenches," but they also occur in other places in the life cycle of a business. There always comes a time when a jump in demand is not met by existing capacity, or when company leadership determines that a jump in capacity is necessary to be able to generate sufficient demand. Scale-up issues are common when the business requires significantly greater numbers of component parts or amounts of raw materials. At some point, the flow of goods, services, human effort, and money into an organization will all require scaling up. Likewise, the flow of products, services, waste, and attrition out of a company will also be scaled up as the company grows.

When Donna must eliminate a bottleneck related to her capacity to meet demand, she faces an issue of scale-up. Her solution is to out-source this business process to several high school students at a rate of $10 per hour, which is less than 25% of what she estimates her own hourly rate to be, before taxes. By scaling up in a flexible man-ner (i.e., using hourly employees, not salaried ones), Donna increases her capacity to meet her surge in demand. Her business also becomes more profitable if she continues to work to her own capacity. However, Donna must consider that hourly and intermittent employees—espe-cially highly skilled labor—require job-specific training and may be more difficult to hire and retain. Donna risks losing these employees if she does not consider providing more consistent income.

Businesses also face issues of scale-back in more pinched economic times. There may be some drawbacks to hiring hourly workers, such as a high turnover rate, increased training and quality control needs, and a possible inability to find help when she needs it in the future. There are also benefits, however, to remaining flexible. She can quickly scale up or scale back capacity. Making investments in nonflexible capacity can prevent a company from being financially solvent. The idle capac-ity that results from expanding human, technological, or equipment-related capacity too quickly can be very expensive. Determining when and how to scale up is a management decision that should take into account the cost, benefits, timing, and potential repercussions of scal-ing up, as well as the personnel decisions related to these activities.

BRAIN PLAY

1. What are the next steps for Donna Johnson on the road to profitability?
2. Think about the last time you went to a supermarket or the Department of Motor Vehicles. What were the bottlenecks? How might these establishments have managed bottlenecks to enhance your service experience?
3. Think about a situation in your personal or professional life where you have experienced a bottleneck. How was this similar to Donna's situation? How did you handle it?

CHAPTER 6

Identifying Non–Value-Added Activities

TODD'S BALANCING ACT

Todd Pearson seeks ways to improve his productivity, both at home and at work. He has a conversation with his wife about ways in which he might eliminate waste from his daily activities. He begins by prioritizing his home life and then takes his new-found enthusiasm to the office.

As you read Todd's story, think about Todd's primary goal. What does he need to accomplish in order to achieve it? What trade-offs must he make?

Todd Pearson's approach to time management was getting him nowhere. As a CPA, vice president, and director of internal audit for a commercial real estate company in Washington, DC, he spent nearly 4 hours a day commuting and exactly that much time fast asleep; he lamented the fact that the amount of time he spent interacting with his two young children averaged only 90 minutes a day. When he factored this into the time he spent in an MBA for Executives program, he feared that if he did not optimize his use of time, his wife, Sarah, would begin to feel left out of his life. Something had to be done, and soon!

Todd began by developing a current-state analysis of his average daily time expenditures in several categories.

Todd's Avg. Day		
Activity		Hours
Sleep		4
Gym		1
Get Ready for Work		1.25
Morning Commute		2
Work (AM)		5.5
Lunch		1
Work (PM)		4
Afternoon Commute		2
Family Time/Dinner		1.25
Put Kids to Bed		0.5
Study		1.5
Total		**24**

TODD'S CURRENT-STATE ANALYSIS OF A TYPICAL DAY.

Then Sarah helped him brainstorm about times of day that contained muda or waste. It helped to have a partner who understood the process and what it meant to him but who still had an objective viewpoint. She knew, for instance, that commuting and getting ready for work were activities he wanted to minimize.

Todd and Sarah also began to prioritize. Increasing his sleep hours was a high priority, for instance, as was spending more time with their children. Sarah pointed out that sleeping and playing with children weren't activities that he could "optimize" in quite the same way: Todd's goal wasn't to be "efficient" at playing but to be more present. On most days, Todd was so exhausted and irritable by the time he arrived home that he was not quite the "fun" dad that he wished he could be. By taking care of himself and being more effective in his work habits, he would be less frazzled and more confident at the end of each day.

In fact, once Todd divided his day into categories, he realized that each activity encapsulated its own metric for optimization. What constituted a successful trip through the "work" portion of his day and how he measured that success were far different from how he measured the success of a commute, a good night's sleep, or a trip to the gym. He needed all of it, but it seemed that the balance between the various segments was most important.

They began looking for creative ways to eliminate obvious areas of waste. The commute was the first thing they tackled. After some research, Todd realized he could cut his commute time in half by leaving home and work earlier.

Todd: I'll have to test this theory out tomorrow, but based on what David says—and his commute is the same as mine—if I leave at 5:30 a.m. instead of 6:45 a.m., I'll cut my morning commute in half. That's an extra hour! And the same thing in the evening—if I leave at 4:30, I can be home by 5:30, based on what I'm hearing from friends. It's like I just won the lottery! Two hours!

Sarah: It's funny—there's a real domino effect. If the first domino is the commute, and we move that piece up here into the 5:30 a.m. slot, we have to do something with your morning gym routine. And the time it takes you to get ready: where can we put that?

Todd: Um ... well, the truth is, I'd like to be able to say that I take full advantage of my lunch hour, but I can't say that at all. Usually I just work through it. If we operate under the assumption that all this Lean and 5S[1] stuff is going to help me become more efficient at managing my workday, let's tentatively say that I'll join a gym close to work and actually go off-site to work out in the middle of the day instead.

Sarah: Great idea, but what do we do with your morning routine?

Todd: Well, we'll have to get into details later, but assuming that we put into practice some fabulous ideas, like making my lunch

---

[1] 5S is a method of organizing, cleaning, developing, and sustaining a more efficient process. The letter S refers to the first letter of five Japanese words often translated as *sort, straighten, shine, standardize,* and *sustain.* This technique will be covered later in the book.

ahead of time and laying out my clothes the night before, we can displace this domino right here in the evening time slot. After putting the kids to bed, maybe we can both spend a half hour preparing the house for the following day, and then we'll both be on the same general schedule.

Sarah: Worth a try, but I'm going to mark in red each activity that needs further attention or definition. We still have to work out the details on that. This is just a rough outline, okay?

Todd: And I still have to study. I probably need more brain power to study than I do to lay out my suit and my lunchbox. We'd better switch those two. I'll prepare after studying and before bedtime.

Sarah: Well, we'll have laundry to fold and the kids' stuff to prepare as well, so that makes sense. And if I have extra time, I can always talk on the phone and watch reality TV. But I think we're on the right track. Let's start with a few of these routine changes and figure out what will need more work.

Todd's rough daily schedule now looked something like this:

Todd's Lean Day		
Activity		Hours
Sleep		7
Get Ready for Work		0.5
Morning Commute		1.0
Work (AM)		4.25
Gym		1.25
Work (AM)		4
Afternoon Commute		1
Family and Dinner		2.5
Put the Kids to Bed		0.5
Study		1.5
Prep for Next Day		0.5
Total		**24**

TODD'S PRELIMINARY ATTEMPT AT SCHEDULE OPTIMIZATION.

Todd knew that this was more of a "desired state" map than a "new normal," but it was worth a try. With the extra time from the reduced commute, he hoped to have almost an hour more with his children. He also hoped to use some of these same techniques at work and become more productive with his work time. Frankly, Todd would have been pleased simply to be happier and more playful when he did spend time with them; to have *more* time to share was an added benefit.

Over the next few weeks, he kept a careful diary of each of the activity zones. Investing in interchangeable clothing and buying lunch food in advance greatly simplified preparing for the next day. At the very least, it was a good excuse to go shopping.

Challenges at work, though, were still a "red zone" for Todd. That 4:30 p.m. departure time was still escaping him, and despite his best efforts, he knew he needed to break apart his work functions and think of creative solutions for managing his time at the office. Early into the second week, he pulled Charlie, his IT manager, into a meeting.

Charlie: How's the new schedule going? Getting here earlier and leaving earlier so you can spend more time with your kids and less time on the road? We think it's brilliant.

Todd: Well, some parts are going well and some parts aren't. Because I'm shifting the times that I'm here, it's getting harder to find out who has the info I need when I'm trying to make decisions. I used to just walk around at certain times of day to gather the reports and updates. I don't want to eliminate walking around—it's the best part of my job, and I need to make regular contact with everyone in the department—but the reporting should all go into a central database so I can get updates as they come in. If I eliminate rushing around for specific information, I can make better use of my time on the floor and leave on time.

Charlie: Well, at my last job we used a shared database that worked really well for this sort of thing. It would house all the relevant documents we needed and allowed everyone to file reports and make updates to projects. If you want to invest in that, it'll take me about a week to set it up and maybe another week to show everyone how to log in, share their updates, and iron out any glitches with the system.

Todd: Amazing, Charlie. Let's do it.

Next, Todd asked his assistant, Ellen, if she would spend a few minutes with him to brainstorm ways they could make their connected offices more efficient. Todd was banking on being able to eliminate some "transportation muda" from his personal space. What he hadn't realized was that Ellen had already come up with a few ideas of her own.

Todd: I was thinking about putting things in standardized places so they're easier to find. Any ideas?

Ellen: Well, the paper and printer ink should be kept next to the printer. Also, I am constantly having to walk around that table, and so are you, so it might be better over there. And then I overheard you talking to Sarah the other day on the phone about your prep time each night, and I was thinking you might want to do the same here—not to say you're not prepared, but shifting some morning activities to the afternoon of the day before might be a good idea.

Todd: Well, I've started writing a to-do list for the next day, and that has helped. When I get in, I already know what's first on the list.

Ellen: While you're at it, the things I need to do for you tend to come in batches or piecemeal throughout the day. If you make another to-do list for me each evening before you leave, that would help me be more efficient, too.

Todd: Good point. I'll see what I can do. It wouldn't hurt for you to get out of here a little earlier, either!

That Friday, following the second full week of Todd's new schedule, he and Sarah celebrated by taking the kids to a two-for-one cheese pizza family night at the local pizza restaurant and arcade. Todd had successfully arrived home between 5:30 p.m. and 5:45 p.m. three nights that week! As astonished as Todd was that things were actually working, he knew he still had some work ahead of him before his system would be the way he wanted it.

"Honey, I'm so proud of you," said Sarah, doling out handfuls of tokens as Todd grabbed some napkins. "The kids won't remember what you bought them as much as what you did with them."

Todd agreed and pointed out that he was happy to be spending more time with her, too. "The funny thing," he added, "is that this kind of change seems to just build on itself. I'm actually starting to get curious about what I can improve next. It's become a kind of game for me."

"Speaking of games," said Sarah, "can you squeeze in a game of Skee-Ball?"

USING LEAN TECHNIQUES TO IMPROVE DAILY ACTIVITIES AND ACHIEVE A GOAL

VALUE-STREAM MAPPING

A *value-stream map* (VSM) is the documentation of the process of creating value for a given product or service. It looks like a flowchart. The VSM begins when a unit of production enters a system and ends when it leaves. For instance, a mill might track a shipment of grain through the process of grinding it into flour, packaging the flour, and transporting the end product. A VSM may be used to identify and separate activities that add value from those that do not, providing a clear picture for making informed improvements such as reduced waste or improved accuracy. A more detailed discussion of the VSM will be provided in "Rebecca's Morning Routine" in Chapter 7.

Lean Takeaways

A successful Lean culture requires meaningful top-line metrics that help all participants identify how their daily decisions help the goals of the organization and meet customer needs. Process improvement principles are meaningless unless they're linked to "top-line metrics," which are not the same for every area of life. In this story, Todd selects "being present and engaged" as his top-line metric and systematically evaluates how he spends his time with regard to this metric. This leads to significant improvements in his productivity by reducing non–value-added activities.

Chapter 7 presents the use of mapping and employee engagement in improving a process.

The "product" that Todd is measuring is himself—specifically, his own energy level. He wants to be able to deliver "himself" to each of his "customers": his wife, children, and coworkers. He and his wife discuss ways he can improve his schedule (an example of a VSM) so that he will have more time to spend with his family in the evenings.

CURRENT- AND FUTURE-STATE ANALYSIS

The *current state* is Todd's description of *what is*, and the *future state* is his best guess at what *could be*. When both are known, he can begin to form trajectories from one to the other. This is easiest to do after Todd has identified his objectives. Then, keeping his objectives in mind, he uses creative solutions such as avoiding rush hour and adjusting other activities to recapture the time and energy he seeks.

Company leaders create a current- and future-state analysis when they establish 5-year plans or quarterly goals. They select ways to measure, define, and monitor their success and then set targets for those metrics. A target can seem far-fetched or even vague—"We plan to double our growth over the next 6 months"—but once the system is mapped, the steps required for execution may become more apparent.

First, the path from the current to the future state should become clear to all involved, and a VSM should be built to describe the current process. Wasteful (non–value-added) activities can be identified and removed from the VSM. Eliminating waste helps to move the current-state VSM in the direction of the desired future-state VSM. Waste identification and removal will be covered in more detail in subsequent chapters.

IDENTIFYING AND REMOVING WASTE

What can Todd's ongoing effort to improve his everyday activities teach us about:

- Value-stream mapping?
- Current- and future-state analysis?
- Identifying and removing muda?
- Top-line metrics?
- Standard work?
- Working smarter, not harder?
- Continuous improvement or kaizen?

Todd identifies two forms of transport waste. By avoiding rush hour, Todd is able to cut his commute in half and save 2 hours a day. By joining a gym within walking distance of his office, he saves an additional hour or so. He converts the 3-hour gain to sleep and recaptures much lost energy. In addition, by laying out his clothes, packing his lunch, and organizing his papers immediately after studying, he eliminates 15 minutes of overprocessing in the morning. This provides an added benefit of more restful sleep. Many small improvement steps can have positive effects elsewhere in the system.

At work, Todd and his assistant rearrange supplies and equipment to better support their needs and eliminate unnecessary motion. Todd creates a shared database, allowing him to retain his walking management style. He then does not need to walk around as often in order to inefficiently gather materials and can focus his real-time interactions with employees on more substantive issues.

TOP-LINE METRICS

Top-line metrics are measurements that stand for, or are composites of, groups of underlying metrics. They serve as broad indicators of success for a set of outcome-oriented activities. Such grouping of metrics allows for a process of elimination when troubleshooting. The source of a problem can be identified and addressed more quickly when a top-line metric is a composite of a discrete set of submetrics.

Todd realizes that he evaluates each segment of his day by a separate set of values. He does not merely seek time with his family; he seeks *quality* time, in terms of energy and attentiveness. At work, he judges his output by different metrics, including revenue growth, employee turnover, and employee effectiveness.

Each of Todd's top-line metrics is an amalgam of many underlying factors. Energy level is a product of exercise, diet, sleep, happiness, and engagement. Work output is a product of data management efficiency, employee engagement and training, and logistics management. Establishing top-line metrics is valuable as a means of setting priorities and communicating them to stakeholders.

STANDARD WORK

Because variability increases the risk of defects, systems can benefit from *standard work*, which is the documented steps in a process, executed the same way every time. This often consists of three components: *takt time*, which is the maximum amount of time an activity can take and still meet the rate of customer demand; *sequencing*, which ensures completion within that time; and *optimum inventory levels*, which keep the process running smoothly. Standard work was introduced in the "Belinda, Bags, and Batches" story (Chapter 4) and will be discussed further in "Rebecca's Morning Routine" in Chapter 7.

Todd's current- and future-state analysis describes standard work. He defines *takt time* when he identifies large categories of activity (such as "prepare for the day") and describes the amount of time required to complete them. He *sequences* tasks when he thinks about sets of individual activities within each category, such as "lay out clothes" or "organize papers." Finally, he considers *optimum inventory* such as lunch supplies and interchangeable clothing to keep his nighttime and morning prep down to a minimum. By monitoring and managing his standard inventory, Todd can eliminate the waste of compensating for shortages.

CONTINUOUS IMPROVEMENT AND KAIZEN

Continuous improvement—*kaizen* in Japanese—assumes that improvement can always be found. In the Japanese tradition, particularly at Toyota, kaizen emphasizes engagement and education of the work force in support of individual contribution. Small improvements not only add value to the business but also provide intangible benefits to employee morale, which can result in greater productivity and lower turnover and attrition rates.

Todd begins his kaizen by involving other stakeholders, including his wife and his administrative assistant. When Todd says to his assistant, "It wouldn't hurt for you to get out of here a little earlier, either" and thinks about batching her tasks, his efforts affect the entire system. Such collaboration is part of the spirit of kaizen.

Two basic tenets of Lean are (1) work smarter, not harder; and (2) don't let perfect get in the way of better. Todd realizes he can get more done in less time each day. He does so by collaborating more effectively with his team and his administrative assistant and when he gains sleep time by avoiding rush hour. The next steps in his Lean journey will be maintaining these gains over the long haul and striving for even more improvements.

BRAIN PLAY

1. What else can Todd do to accomplish his goals of improving his life at work and at home and achieving greater effectiveness in all areas of his life?
2. How could an elementary school use some of these same techniques to improve its productivity, including value-stream mapping, current- and future-state definition, identifying and eliminating muda, top-line metrics, or standard work?
3. Think about a situation in your personal or professional life where the use of Lean tools would be appropriate. What are the barriers to conducting an analysis similar to Todd's and acting upon it? Briefly describe how you would address each of the implementation steps.

CHAPTER 7

Mapping the Value Stream

REBECCA'S MORNING ROUTINE

Rebecca Tilden had primary custody of her children, Jackson, age 7, and Wyatt, age 5; her boys lived with her 6 days out of 7. After graduating with an MBA in 2003, Rebecca established her own program development consultancy, Tilden Consulting. Because her children were both still young and needed extra support, the flexibility of working for individual clients was essential. Without another adult at home to pitch in, long nights at the office simply weren't an option.

Rebecca Tilden works with her children to come to a group consensus on the best way to approach the tasks that occur on a given school day. The family identifies and evaluates each task to perform between arriving home in the early evening and stepping onto the school bus the next morning.

As you read Rebecca's story, think about what choices she and her family made to create more effective and enjoyable mornings and evenings.

With so much to accomplish in any given day and a structure imposed by her boys' schooling, Rebecca needed to be able to plan her time down to 15-minute intervals. She was committed to being present and available to her children when she was with them, yet she also needed the ability to respond quickly to customer requests and produce top-quality material on time and above expectation.

Most of the hours in Rebecca's days were carefully planned, and she enjoyed the variety and complexity of her work. What she found most difficult were morning and evening routines with the children. It was an uphill battle; she was constantly repeating each direction five or six times, and her boys found every possible reason to avoid or delay basic daily activities such as brushing their teeth, picking up clothes or dishes, and packing their lunches and backpacks. Often, after 10 hours in school and at child care, they were simply too tired to focus on much of anything.

Fortunately, one of Rebecca professors was an expert in everyday applications of Lean thinking. He encouraged her to formally apply a process-flow map to both her morning and evening routines—and to engage the boys in the process as she did so.

One weekday evening, Rebecca and her sons were in the kitchen. They had just finished dinner, and the boys were getting up from the table and clearing the dinner dishes.

Rebecca: Okay, guys, listen up. I'm calling a family meeting.

Jackson: But Mom, I want to go play.

Wyatt: Me too!

Rebecca: Boys, I need your help. This is important, and besides, it's raining outside. Sit back down, and each of you take some of these index cards and a pencil.

Wyatt: I can't write.

Rebecca: Yes, you can. I'll help you.

MT '11

Wyatt: Okay! [*He grabs a stack of cards.*]

Jackson: Where's my pencil?

Rebecca [hands Jackson a pencil]: This is what the meeting is about. I want you to write down everything you do between the time I pick you up at after-school care all the way to the next morning, when I'm walking you to the bus stop.

Jackson: Write down when I walk to the bus stop?

Wyatt: Mom, I'm too tired. I can't do it.

Rebecca: Yes, you can, Wyatt. I've seen you do it. Now listen, boys. I want you to write down what we do so you understand how we're going to change our mornings and evenings.

Jackson: Why?

Rebecca: Good question, sweetie. Do you guys like hearing Mommy get upset when you aren't ready for school on time in the morning?

Wyatt: No. You're mean.

Rebecca: Well, I don't want to be mean, honey, but I get frustrated when we do things at the last minute. And do you guys like feeling so tired in the morning? Wyatt, don't you cry almost every morning because you don't like it when I ask you to rush?

Wyatt: Because you're mean.

Jackson: She has to be mean because we're not ready on time.

Rebecca: I'm not—Wyatt, I'm going to help you. We need to sit here as a family and write down everything that needs to get done, and then we'll decide what pile each card goes in. Actually, first, how will we know if what we're doing is working to help us with our routine? How will we know if we did it right?

Jackson: Well, we will be all ready for the bus at the exact right time, and we won't have to run around trying to put our coats and shoes on or leave the house without our homework or without brushing our teeth.

Rebecca: Great, honey! Okay, what are the things we should be writing on our cards?

Wyatt: Put on shoes!

Jackson: Brush teeth! At night and in the morning!

MT '11

Wyatt: Eat breakfast!

Rebecca: Great job, boys! Put one idea on each card, and I'll write my own ideas too.

Boys: Okay! [*They get to work, asking for help occasionally with spelling. By the end, they have a huge stack of activities.*]

Rebecca: Okay, here's what we're going to do next. Let's make different piles for the different routines that we need. There's the "walking in the door" routine, the "homework and dinnertime" routine, the "get ready for tomorrow" routine, and the "bedtime" routine. The last one is the "get ready for school" routine.

Jackson: That's a lot of routines, Mommy.

Wyatt: Mommy, I can put my shoes on before I go to bed—then I will already have them on when I wake up!

Rebecca: Sweetie, that's a great idea, but shoes are not for beds. We want to make sure we do things in the best order. Sometimes there's a reason for doing things later, and sometimes there's not. I like your idea of doing certain activities the night before. Jackson, what should go in the "walking in the door" routine?

Jackson: Um, take your shoes off and put your bag away?

Wyatt: What about your lunchbox?

Jackson: Yeah, okay, your lunchbox.

Rebecca: And your folder, too, I think. [*Shuffling through the index cards.*] You can play a little bit right after school before we get into your homework, but I want you to take out your folder and lay it out on this table before you go play. So that's four things. [*She places them in one column.*] Shoes off and in the basket, folder out on the table, empty lunchbox, and put your bag by the front door.

Wyatt: Are we done yet?

Rebecca: Almost done, sweetie, almost done. Now, on the days you go to after-school care, they do some of your homework with you. But I still need to check it because sometimes they miss something. And Jackson, I want to help you study for your tests. So even on those days, we'll have a little homework.

Jackson: Okay, so that card goes here, and then after that we can put dinnertime and clear your place.

Wyatt: And say prayers!

Rebecca [feeling virtuous to have such stellar children]: Sure, Wyatt, we can put all that in the homework and dinnertime pile. And after dinner, if there's a little time, you can go play for a while so I can clean up.

Jackson: I can do the dishes, Mommy!

Rebecca: Oh, you are so sweet, honey, but you need some playtime too, between the homework and dinner routine and the get-ready-for-tomorrow routine. So you guys can play while I clean up, and then I'll help you while you do the things in **this** pile. [*She gestures to the next pile, which is ready to be sorted into a column.*]

Wyatt: Well, Mommy, I want to pack my lunch and my snack.

Rebecca: Great sweetie, you guys will both pack your lunches and snacks! And then you can lay out your clothes for the next day.

Jackson: Mommy, Wyatt always cries in the morning when you make him put his shoes on. He never likes the socks, and he always waits until the last minute.

Rebecca: Great observation, Jackson. We'll have to think about that. Wyatt, how do you think you can make the way you put your shoes on **better**?

Jackson: **What** operation?

Rebecca: **Observation**, honey. Something that you noticed. In this case, you noticed something we can improve together that will help everybody. That's why I told you it was great!

Wyatt: I can put my shoes on before I go to bed, Mommy. I already **told** you.

Rebecca: Sweetie, your body needs all of its parts, even your feet, to be loose so your body can do all of its repairing and growing at night. But what if you put on your shoes before you leave your bedroom to come and eat breakfast?

Wyatt: Okay, Mommy, when I lay out my clothes the night before I can lay my shoes there, too, instead of putting them next to the front door.

Rebecca: Perfect! Great! I am so proud of you for thinking of that!

Jackson: So, Wyatt, let's put another card here in the get-ready-for-tomorrow column that says "Lay Out Shoes and Socks." I'll make another card for us.

Wyatt: Are we done?

Rebecca: Okay, okay. The last column for nighttime is the go-to-bed pile. You have to brush your teeth, put on pajamas, and then I'll read you each your own book for special time. Then it's lights out, with the door open, okay?

Jackson: Okay, let's do the last Colin, Mommy.

Rebecca: It's *column*, sweetie: a line down, from top to bottom, with things in it, like these cards that we made. I'll put them on a board on the wall when we're finished. The last one is the go-to-school routine. What's first, Wyatt?

Wyatt: Wake up. Go to the bathroom. Put my clothes and shoes on all together.

Rebecca: Great! Good job!

Jackson: Then we eat breakfast and get ready to go.

Rebecca: Well, you do *eat* breakfast next. But after you eat it, you have to pick up your dishes, remember? [*The boys nod.*] And then you do a bag check. That means you put your snack, lunch-box, and homework folder in your bag. I need to look in the folder to make sure there's nothing for me to sign or fill out for the school.

Wyatt: And then we need our coats and hats and all that!

Rebecca: Yup, that's the last thing. You guys get your coats on, or hats, or whatever you need for the weather, and put your bag on. Then we can all start walking! Yay!

Jackson: Mommy, this is a lot of stuff. Look at all these things.

Rebecca: That's why I wanted you guys to see it all. I want you to under-stand that I'm not just reminding you to do the same things over and over again because it's fun for me. I'm reminding you because there are so many things that we have to do together.

Wyatt: Mommy, I like it when you read to me at night. That's my favor-ite one here. And dinner.

Rebecca: Well, yes, sweetie, I like those things too! And I like to be able to sit down with you when you're eating, instead of using that time to clean up. So the better we get at doing all of these things in the routines, the more time Mommy will have to hang out with you guys.

Jackson: Okay, Mom, well, can we go play now?

Rebecca: Sure. We'll try out the new routines after your playtime, when we start getting ready for tomorrow, okay?

[*Wyatt and Jackson hug their mom and run off to play with the train set upstairs.*]

USING CRITICAL PATH AND VALUE-STREAM MAPPING TO ESTABLISH STANDARD WORK AT HOME

Lean Takeaways

Converting a chaotic current-state situation into a desired future state that is calm, collected, and ultimately more productive requires application of the Lean activities of value-stream mapping and standard work. Rebecca and her children create a set of expectations for the family by establishing consistent processes so they know what is required of each of them. Acceptance and adherence to these expectations are stronger because of the collective development process.

The next story will introduce a new framework for streamlining processes and activities and go into more detail on the concept of standard work.

CRITICAL PATH

The "critical path" determines the amount of time required to perform a given task. Improving the activities on the critical path can reduce the completion time of the entire task. Reducing the time of a critical activity will shorten the time of an entire task; reducing the elapsed time of a noncritical activity has no effect on the time of an entire task. A critical path analysis enables us to focus on those activities that have the *greatest* impact on the completion time, in effect the bottlenecks. This will allow for focused monitoring and targeted improvement efforts.

Rebecca and her family have several objectives. The primary objective in the morning is for both children to catch the school bus with everything they need in their bags, on their feet, and in their stomachs. If these activities do not occur, then the morning is deemed a "defect" and corrective action must be taken: the children must be delivered to school by car and Rebecca is late for work, for example, or someone is unprepared or hungry. The minimum requirement for a successful morning is that there must always be enough time to complete the critical path. Certainly there are other requirements, such as happy children or a tear-free morning—but these are not the minimum requirements for the critical path.

Another example of the critical path is real estate development. A building is not saleable or rentable until it is in turnkey condition, and many of the activities are sequential (i.e., they are dependent on one another). For instance, the walls cannot be built unless the foundation is poured, the roof cannot be added unless there is something upon which to build it, and the floors cannot be sanded until the walls are repaired and painted. While some of the activities can be prepared in advance or concurrently (such as factory-made walls), many of the requirements of construction occur in sequence and are dependent upon one another. Therefore, these sequential activities define the critical path, which in turn determines the time for successful completion.

VALUE-STREAM MAP (VSM)

A value-stream map (VSM) charts the activities in a process to visualize the flow of materials and information. A VSM separates those activities that add value from those that do not. A VSM also separates activity time from actual processing time. It may take Rebecca's children 60 minutes to get out of the house in the morning, yet the actual time spent "doing" things may be only 35—and of that 35 minutes, 10 may be unnecessary. Rebecca's VSM can also assist in identifying overprocessing waste. Overprocessing is performing extra steps in a process that are above and beyond the customer's requirements. For example, Rebecca might find that Jackson brushes his teeth both before and after breakfast, which isn't necessary.

VSMs are also covered in "Todd's Balancing Act" (Chapter 6). Todd maps his energy and effectiveness throughout his day. In this story, Rebecca creates a VSM of "the children" as each activity of their morning (getting dressed, eating breakfast, and putting on shoes and socks) and adds slightly more "value" to the finished product. The finished product is "children ready for school and on the school bus."

How can we learn from Rebecca's family's approach to managing their daily tasks before and after school in the following areas:

- Critical path?
- Value-stream maps?
- Culture?

CULTURE

How might a manager hold a meeting to introduce continuous process improvement tools for the first time? Employees must understand the process and their place in moving along the critical path. Involving employees in the planning of their actions toward meeting a shared goal not only makes compliance more likely, but also increases awareness of the personal benefits of teamwork and process improvement. Rebecca and her sons hold a kickoff meeting similar to one that an operations manager might hold.

As Continuous Process Improvement (CPI) activities become ingrained, they can evolve as part of an organization's culture. Companies like Starbucks or Trader Joe's hire and develop people who want to be part of a spirited team and are enthusiastic about serving customers. This is because customer service and relationship management are often central to a company's value proposition and competitive advantage. While Rebecca cannot select her children, she certainly can provide a nurturing and supportive environment, and opportunities to learn and grow. Employers who honor internal stakeholders as earnestly as they do external stakeholders tend to attract engaged employees. Culture, when viewed in the context of a Lean implementation, is at least as important as the actual process improvements or waste reductions.

BRAIN PLAY

1. What else can Rebecca and her family do to accomplish their goal of improving the morning and evening transition times?
2. How could an airline that is focused on improving turnaround times use some of these same techniques? (Critical path, value-stream mapping, standard work, and employee engagement?)
3. Think about a situation in your personal or professional life where the use of these Lean tools would be appropriate. Briefly describe each of the implementation steps.

CHAPTER 8

Establishing Standard Work

ERIKA, IN THROUGH THE OUT DOOR

Erika Deibert lived alone in a three-story townhouse with a first-floor garage. An intelligent and successful executive in the health care consulting industry, she liked her job and was good at it. She felt efficient while in the office but also enjoyed being at home, where she could retreat from the hectic world outside, catch up on work, entertain friends, and sleep.

Erika Deibert organizes her home with an eye to simplifying and standardizing her processes. She uses a standard 5S approach for creating and optimizing an entry-exit hub for her home and to her morning coffee routine.

As you read Erika's story, think about what factors she considers and the choices she makes when redesigning her kitchen and entry-exit hub.

She lived simply and well, managing to limit her furnishings to a few simple yet functional pieces. A maid came once a week to vacuum, mop, and clean the bathrooms and kitchen. This was hardly necessary, since Erika often ate out for both lunch and dinner; the most she would prepare for herself was toast and coffee for breakfast and a salad in the evening. It was truly a life centered on work, socializing, relaxation— and the avoidance of accumulation.

Erika did allow herself to accumulate shoes. She tended to match shoes with outfits and owned about 75 pairs in all—five for every suit she owned. The shoe pile was an enormous heap of leather and laces; she often found herself pawing through a pile of stilettos, muttering under her breath about the scrapes and bruises she sustained as a result. She could never find the ones she wanted when she wanted them. This was a constant source of irritation.

The other unfortunate bump on Erika's otherwise smooth road was the process of bringing in and sorting the mail. It seemed that the mountain of junk mail would never abate—no sooner would she devote 15 minutes of precious time to deciding which trash can should receive the newest holiday catalogs and insurance company mailings than another batch would clog her mailbox. Overall, Erika's life was rather streamlined, but not everything was working.

One day, curled up on her cozy chaise longue, Erika considered how she had worked hard to get to a place in her life where she could enjoy the finer things, and then pondered how she might address those areas that still annoyed her. She decided to rectify the shoe and mail problems immediately.

Erika determined that what required attention were the interfaces between activities outside and inside her home on a typical day. Her morning coffee ritual was also in need of restructuring. Once she had made it through the office door or settled in at home, everything was fine; what needed a makeover were the transitions, the "shift change," the setup required to run another batch. The edges of things.

MT '11

Once Erika identified the routines she wanted to optimize, doing so was a breeze. She converted a bathroom on the landing between her first-floor garage and the second-floor main living space into a "shoe room," taking full advantage of standard storage products. Now she had a place for not only every pair of shoes but also umbrellas, coats, bags, and other weather-related accessories. She also thought to install a table next to an outlet where she could charge her smartphone and also drop her keys and ID badge. It was a dream; she now had a complete entry-exit hub to manage the trappings of her comings and goings.

The mail, too, was rather simple, once she dealt with the problem head-on instead of continuing to allow it to annoy her and drain her energy. The first thing Erika did was install a large recycling bin in her entry-exit hub that allowed her to discard much of her incoming mail before it even entered her main living space. Second, she set aside a few hours to research ways to remove herself from the many mailing lists that she'd been added to over time. She found a service online whereby, for $25, she could provide the junk mail that she'd collected for three months, and the company would do the grunt work of getting her off the lists. That sounded worth the gamble, so she decided to let the catalogs accumulate and then send in the whole pile.

Erika's morning kitchen routine, however, required a bit more attention. The shoe room and junk mail solutions were examples of kaizen[1]
events, but her morning routine cried out for a full-bore Lean process
improvement campaign. Not a morning person, Erika would walk in
circles around the kitchen multiple times, grabbing coffee on one pass,
a piece of toast on another, and perhaps a disposable lid along the third
lap, all before beginning the task of identifying the perfect shoes.

Of all her tasks, this was the most difficult to improve; yet through
some ingenuity and a small capital investment, she solved the problem.
Now, in her caffeine-deprived state, she would stand in one place and
select a flavor from her instant, single-serve coffee maker, take three
steps to the next cabinet to choose a cup, then arrive at the brewer to
drop her flavor selection into the machine and press "brew." Instead of
padding around the Italian tile as her coffee brewed, she took her vita-
mins. "Boring," she reflected, as she popped a probiotic capsule, capped
her freshly brewed cup, and headed downstairs to the "hub."

---

[1] Kaizen is the idea of continual improvement of a process, and of every step in the
process, through relentless evaluation. Kaizen "events" are often short bursts of
activity whose goal is a specific improvement project.

While driving to the office, she realized she'd shaved nearly 20 minutes off her morning routine, then instantly calculated what that meant in terms of incrementally accumulated beauty sleep over the next 15 years. *Ah*, she sighed to herself as she coasted to a stop: *The true meaning of "value-add."*

STANDARDIZING WORK TO REDUCE CYCLE TIME IN THE KITCHEN AND ENTRYWAY

5S

5S is a method for organizing an underfunctioning space. Each "S" signifies one of the following steps: sort, straighten, shine, standardize, and sustain. *Sorting* involves reducing the number of items by removing those that are unnecessary—shoes that are out of style or that no longer fit, for example, or duplicate items that have accumulated unnecessarily. Food in a refrigerator might be sorted into "good" and "bad," and discarded accordingly.

Lean Takeaways

Using 5S, Erika removes non–value-added activities (such as searching for shoes) from her morning routine—reducing muda such as overprocessing, excess motion, excess transport, and defects. By standardizing her routines, she has time and resources. A repeatable process has many benefits, such as enabling a more accurate time forecast and simplified improvement opportunities.

The next story, in Chapter 9, will expand on each step of the 5S process.

Straightening involves arranging the remaining items so the most frequently used are more easily accessible and so that transport, motion, and search time are minimized. Everyday shoes are stored in the front of the closet, for example, while infrequently used dress shoes are placed further back. The steps of *sort* and *straighten*, taken together, reduce clutter by first removing unwanted or unneeded items and then finding appropriate places for the items that remain.

Shining (or *sweeping*) a space is more than just cleaning up; it's discovering how and why clutter or disorder have accumulated and taking corrective steps. The *shining* step sometimes requires adding new things rather than just the elimination that often occurs in the process of *sorting* and *straightening*. The next grocery list, for example, might contain some new foods to fill out the recently emptied space on the second shelf; a heavy closet cleaning might cause the wardrobe owner to realize the need for a new pair of black shoes that complements his dark suit collection; or, at a business, a new rack might be purchased to make a closet full of maintenance equipment more usable to the operator. The key is not to expect a large investment for infrastructure if the *sorting* step has been taken, because usually there is less need for storage space once unnecessary items have been removed.

Standardizing is a refinement step that makes the process so intuitive that a checklist is no longer needed. It is a precursor to the last step, *sustain*, which is the process of repeating or scaling up the system and maintaining it over time. *Standardizing* might mean creating a manual that defines a filing system, but *sustaining* means teaching the filing system to others and ensuring that the files are monitored and reviewed. *Sustaining* is the process of maintaining the gains produced by the first four steps, and it is the step that achieves and creates the "new normal"—the new current state.

As Erika performs a 5S analysis on several of her household functional areas, she keeps in mind the outcome or purpose of the spaces. Each location (kitchen and entry-exit hub) plays a critical role in Erika's daily routines, which should in turn support Erika's life goals. The set of processes (standard work) that Erika determines for *using* her spaces is not the same thing as the 5S process. The five steps in the 5S process are specifically used to optimize *space*, whereas standard work describes the *processes that will take place within that space*. These are distinct but related concepts. Being able to visualize the end result and knowing how each component of that end state adds value should influence the decisions she makes.

In the kitchen, Erika *sorts* and *straightens* by eliminating non–value-added objects and then categorizing what remains. She considers why her kitchen became problematic for her to use in the first place (the *shine* step). She realizes that she can reduce the re-accumulation of non–value-added items in her kitchen by adding a new single-serve cup coffee maker and purchasing and storing her vitamin jars in easy reach of the coffee machine. She considers the ways she uses the space (standard work) and relates these to the physical organization and available equipment in the kitchen area. Erika then *standardizes* by keeping her kitchen clean and stocking her shelves with supplies. Finally, Erika *sustains* the process through practice. By this point, Erika should be able to simply hand over a simple manual to any new household employee that explains the organization of the kitchen, the tasks that must be performed to maintain the space as is, and the reasons for the choices she has made.

In the new entry-exit hub, Erika *sorts* and *straightens* by eliminating items that clutter the space and organizing items that she does want. She creates places to sort mail, keep her keys and ID card, and store weather-related items such as coats and umbrellas and, of course, shoes! In the *shine* step, Erika will be sure that the area is clean, and that it retains its functionality.

As Erika uses the room, she may notice certain aspects of the way the space is organized that should be adjusted. This is the *standardize* portion of the 5S process. The *standardize* step is the result of the interaction between the standard work processes and the space that has been designed to support them. Perhaps she realizes that a few pairs of shoes she uses more often must be shifted downward, or that one shoe collection would be easier to select from if it were sorted by heel height or color. Erika *standardizes* when she works out the kinks and defines the process so that she would feel comfortable handing a manual about her mudroom to a new employee. Lastly, she *sustains* her improvements by keeping the room clean and remembering to empty the recycle bins so her junk mail doesn't overflow the bin. One of the primary indications of a successful 5S implementation is minimizing the effort required to *sustain* it.

KAIZEN

Kaizen is a Japanese term for "continuous process improvement" or CPI. The philosophy is that things can always be improved, as opposed to only fixing things when they are broken. Kaizen was also discussed in Chapter 6, "Todd's Balancing Act."

How can Erika's approach to redesigning her space provide us with insights into:

- 5S?
- Kaizen?
- Identifying and eliminating muda?
- Standard work?
- Cycle time, takt time, and standard inventory?

While kaizen is often thought of as a long-term, holistic process, the same concepts can be used to improve an isolated process. In Erika's case, she already has a very streamlined life, and she wants to use the kaizen model to reorganize her home and the routines that mark her transitions between one set of activities (inside the house) and another (outside the house). She is still using the kaizen model, however, by being proactive and finding ways to think critically about and improve a process before it is "broken." We do not follow Erika's life long enough to see what she does with the increase in energy that she might have after her new routines have been in effect for a while; it is likely that her smoother experiences of leaving and arriving home will free up time and attention that she can put to use elsewhere. While she may simply spend more time relaxing with friends or watching television, it's also possible that Erika will use her "extra" time for some other productive activity. Similarly, as a company makes investments in streamlined, aligned processes and builds employee capability—and as the benefits from these projects begin to compound and become more noticeable—the company can also become more profitable.

IDENTIFYING AND REMOVING MUDA

Muda is a Japanese word that means *waste*, which is understood to be anything that does not add value. The eight categories of muda are as follows:

- Transportation
- Excess inventory
- Motion
- Waiting or queuing
- Overproduction
- Overprocessing
- Mistakes (defects)
- Untapped creativity or human potential

Erika has already streamlined much of her workday, wardrobe, household management, and career. She is satisfied with her life but identifies

---

BRAIN PLAY

1. What could Erika do to further improve her productivity at home?
2. How could a legal practice that is focused on turning around important documents with high levels of accuracy use the philosophy of 5S and standard work?
3. Think about a situation in your personal or professional life where the use of these Lean tools would be appropriate. Briefly describe the implementation steps.

---

areas to improve. Her new mail- and coat-room (entry-exit hub) eliminates excess motion, transportation, and overprocessing; her kitchen organization eliminates excess motion and waiting; and her shoe closet, located in the entry-exit hub, eliminates the overprocessing of searching for the correct pair of shoes.

CHAPTER 9

Implementing the 5S System

DAVID AND THE CASE
OF THE HOARDED HOUSE

David and his wife, Heidi, had lived in their single-family home in a new development for about a year and a half. Both followed hectic schedules: David was a student in an MBA for Executives program and a full-time IT program manager, and Heidi was the executive director of a local performing arts center, which required her to work odd hours. As a result, the two of them had allowed their home to accumulate layer upon layer of stuff in almost every room, closet, and wardrobe.

David throws his hands up at the uselessness of his cluttered house and resolves to address his hoarding problem. Heidi, his wife, is overjoyed at his focus on reclaiming their shared space, and they work together to bring order and usefulness to their cabinets, closet, and garage.

At what point in the 5S process do David and Heidi make the most critical decisions? What makes these steps so important?

One night in December, David drove home from an evening class as a wintry mix of snow and freezing rain began to accumulate on the street. Their house had an attached garage, but he and his wife typically parked on the street and used the front door, because the garage still held a large number of unpacked boxes from their recent move. The wind had picked up, and David was tired, hungry, and cold, so, feeling ambitious, he decided to test the garage entry to his home.

He was not sure whether the batteries in the garage door opener were going to work, but when he pressed the button, the garage door began to lift. He slowly nosed his car into the garage, hoping for the best, but there were simply too many boxes. He moved the car to the curb, carefully navigated the sidewalk to the front door, sank into the living room couch, and called his wife at work.

David: Look at how ridiculous it is outside, and I had to park on the street. I have sleet down my shirt. Our garage is worthless.

Heidi: And how was your day? Mine was great. Thanks for asking.

David: Oh, sorry. I'm tired.

Heidi: I agree; I'd like to park in the garage on a night like this, too. What do you say we clean out the whole house? I think we need to admit that we have a problem.

David: You mean with unpacking?

Heidi: No, I mean we are hoarders, David. Not first-rate hoarders like on that reality show or anything—I know I throw away most of the holiday cards we get every year—but we are just too lazy to go through our stuff and clean it up. Simple as that.

David: Well, they do say that admitting you have a problem is the first step.

Heidi: Put something on the stove, will you? I'm leaving now; I'll see you soon.

[*A half hour later, Heidi swings through the front door and practically runs into David, who is still sprawled out on the couch. She plants herself next to him and leans in for a hug.*]

Heidi: Hi, honey. Doesn't look like we're very close to eating dinner, huh?

David: Well, no. I've been thinking about what you said, and I'm completely overwhelmed by all the stuff in this house. I admit it, you're right. We're hoarders!

Heidi: Well, no time like the present. Let's order a pizza and then make a list; that's always the best place to start. [*She whips out a mini legal pad and begins to write.*] I'm going to start by identifying and prioritizing the areas in our home that need help:

1. Garage
2. Pantry
3. Closet
4. Office
5. Laundry room

And, as much as I love you, the tools and equipment in the garage are all yours. If you haul those unpacked boxes into the house, I can sort through them and see if there's anything of value. Frankly, if we don't even remember what's in there after 18 months, I'm not convinced it would really matter if we gave them away unopened. Just in case it's your mother's antique silver, I'll take a peek. But the tools are yours.

David: Sure, that seems like as good a place as any to start. That way, we can at least park inside now that the weather's cold!

Three weeks later, David returned home from the same late-night executive education class as the fated night of his epiphany. He confidently pressed the button on the garage door opener, parked easily in the garage, and looked around to view the work he and his wife had done over the past weeks. The lighting was bright, and the space was clear and organized. Heidi and he had ended up going through everything together. Half of the tools and hardware that David had hung on to for most of his adult life had been discarded or donated; the rest had been categorized and either sorted into a set of heavy-duty drawers or hung on the wall. He got out of the car easily and walked proudly into the kitchen.

Once inside, he could see that Heidi was home unusually early and had begun a project that could only be described as ambitious. The pantry had been emptied onto the kitchen table, and she had begun to sort through the resulting mountain of packaged goods.

David [kissing his wife on the cheek and plopping onto the couch]: That garage is a killer. I can actually imagine working in there. And the car actually fits without breaking anything! How was your day?

Heidi: Great! Now that the garage turned out so well, I couldn't wait to get home and empty the pantry so I could start on this project.

David: Did you just say what I think you said?

Heidi: You just said it yourself: That garage rocks. I want a pantry that is equally rockin'.

David: Okay. What can I do to help?

Heidi [passing him the spice rack]: You can go through the spices.

David: What's the criteria?

Heidi: Well, instead of focusing on keeping everything that we "might" need someday, I'm only keeping the stuff we're using right now. Anything that's expired is an automatic toss. Any foods we haven't eaten in the last 6 months go over there, to be given to a food bank. I've eliminated 30 percent already. Going for half.

David: Are you sure you aren't throwing away something we might need?

Heidi: We can put the bags in the garage for a few days, so if we miss anything, we can still get it. Otherwise, I'd rather get rid of it and risk having to buy it again.

David: Just think how much more efficient our lives will be with an empty pantry. It'll be much easier to convince you to go out to a restaurant, because we won't have anything left!

Heidi: Actually, I think we'll end up cooking more because it will be so much easier to find what we need. Look around this kitchen! We have so much food that we didn't even remember we had.

David: I suppose we should eat our way through a good part of what's left before we go out to a restaurant again.

Heidi: This, of course, raises the question: "How did we get into such a mess in the first place?"

David: I think we need some sort of system to limit the amount of stuff we have. Why do we have four jars of chili powder?

Heidi: Well every time you make your firehouse chili, you buy more. Or, you think that we don't have any because you can't find it in the pantry.

David: Yeah, but my chili rocks! At school, we learned about visual management and something called a *kanban*. I think it may apply here.

Heidi: Go on.

David: Well, first, a kanban is meant to go with the 5S system—everything in a set place. When things are organized visually, it becomes apparent when we run out or need more of an item. The other part of a kanban has to do with inventory that can be easily seen and assessed.

For instance, let's say we have two jars of peanut butter, one behind the other in the pantry. Each jar is in its established place. When one jar gets used, the other jar takes its place and the empty space is a signal, or kanban, for us to add peanut butter to the grocery list.

Because the physical space to store the peanut butter is limited, it both prevents us from buying too much and provides a signal to buy more when it is empty. When we use a kanban, we are "pulling" our peanut butter inventory rather than "pushing" it.

Heidi: OK. That should work for many of our pantry items—maybe toilet paper and paper towels? Or yogurt—that seems to be a food group around here.

Let me get through this process and see what we're left with. I want to clean the shelves, categorize the food that's left, and designate a category for each shelf so it's easier to find stuff. Then I'll do the same thing with the drawers and keep only the utensils and appliances we actually use at least every once in a while. Things we use frequently should go on the countertop. Fix or replace whatever needs it, that kind of thing. Get the space so that you want to work in it. Maybe put in some better lighting.

David: Then what?

Heidi: Well, a volunteer has been coming to work to help us get organized, and she has been talking about five steps. After *sort* and *straighten* comes *shine*—cleaning the space. But it's more than just cleaning; it's figuring out how and why things get as bad as they do. Like letting the dishes pile up. We never have any clean pans. We can't find anything, so we have to dig around to find stuff, and then we leave things out. That kind of thing. So my next step is to observe *how* we do things so I can figure out what we *need* to do.

David: I suppose we could put things directly in the dishwasher.

Heidi: What a concept.

David: I think half the time we are just adding more dishes to the pile to see which one of us will break down and clean them first.

MT. '11

Heidi: We can try that. Then the next step is *standardize*—see the pattern?

David: I know—we use that system in the exec ed class also.

Heidi: Well, you could have mentioned that!

David: I just wanted to see how much you knew. [*Heidi glares at him.*] Well, I'm an equal partner in this mess. I'll do it with you. Seriously, though, I am wondering how you interpret the *standardize* step.

Heidi: It's the step where you try to eliminate checklists. The work processes that take place at each workstation should be so intuitive that you don't need endless lists to remind you. It's a refinement step—you start developing standards to maintain. In the kitchen, we cook, eat, and clean. I want to do all three easily, and if possible, I want them to be fun. I want them to be a seamless, effortless part of our day. But if we don't have a target, then we won't know when we're hitting or missing.

David: You mean, we have to pay attention. [*Heidi throws a wet rag at him, which he deflects into the sink.*] Hit the target. Okay, what about *sustain*?

Heidi: It's just about seeing how well you've done the previous four steps. If you go through the steps correctly, then sustaining your changes should be easy.

David: This has been a great review: ops begins at home!

Heidi: Of course, now that we're so excited to make dinner at home more, I ordered pizza.

David: A woman after my own heart. Just for that, I'll take those bags to the food bank tomorrow.

Heidi: While you're doing that, there are also five huge bags of clothes ready for Goodwill.

David: Where'd it all come from?

Heidi: Well, you won't believe it, but I organized our closet.

David: Hey—what did you take?

Heidi: Don't worry, it's mostly my stuff, except for a few of your ties. I want to see if you notice which ones are missing.

[*David goes to the closet, and Heidi follows.*]

David: The fish tie is missing, but that's okay.

Heidi: So what do you think of my side?

David [*sees that half the clothing is gone*]: Wow. Impressive.

Heidi: I decided that if I haven't worn it in over a year, it should go. And some of it was just worn out or out of style.

David: So how do you know you aren't going to just fill it up again with new clothes? Or is that the plan?

Heidi: No—I do like to shop, but that might be part of the standardize step: identifying what might get in the way of keeping this space organized and functional.

David: You could have a rule that if you bring home something new, it has to replace something else. Keep the number of articles of clothing constant.

Heidi [reluctantly]: I could try that.

David: You could always try the tie approach: take things out to the garage, then after a month, look at what you've gotten rid of. If you really want it back, return it to the closet. Otherwise, Goodwill.

Heidi: I'll have to think about that.

David: The pizza will be here any minute. Let's go clean out the rest of the pantry. No time like the present.

Heidi: A man after my own heart!

CREATING TIME AND FUNCTIONALITY WITH 5S

5S

The 5S system guides the organization of physical space so it functions for the intended purpose. In Chapter 8, Erika Deibert uses 5S to organize her entry-exit hub and her kitchen. In this chapter, David and Heidi use the 5S system in their kitchen, garage, and closet to eliminate clutter and create more organized, usable spaces. They alter their habits so that the clutter, once eliminated, does not return. Last, they establish new routines and

Lean Takeaways

By rigorously applying the steps of Lean 5S, and the *sort* and *sustain* steps above all, David and Heidi are able to organize their storage space and make it usable again. A structured process such as 5S is useful in this context to make the best use of space and tools.

This concludes the section on capability; the next several chapters and their stories move into the third of the "Five Cs": control. Now that we understand how to make the most of our existing resources, we can apply new techniques to improving the reliability and consistency of our processes.

standardize them, including rethinking their process for buying new supplies or items, which is called a kanban system. Standard work and kanban systems will be discussed in this chapter.

STANDARD WORK

As with some of our previous protagonists, David and Heidi spend some of their time establishing "standard work." Their existing life had been "normal," as in "That's the way we normally do things." However, that normal was a "suboptimal" normal, with nonrepeatable processes, time spent looking for items, duplicate items, and general disarray. Their goal, through the 5S system and the establishment of standard work, was to develop a new normal—a "better" normal.

Their "new normal," through the *standardize* and *sustain* phases of 5S, establishes standard work in the areas of inventory supply replenishment and clothing purchases. They establish standard work by placing dishes directly into the dishwasher and create rules for discarding unneeded items.

KANBAN

Kanban is a visual inventory management system. The word *kanban* combines the Japanese words for card and signal, *kan* and *ban*. Kanban is a central element of Lean manufacturing and is probably the most widely used type of pull-signaling system. David and Heidi create a rudimentary kanban system when they arrange their pantry supplies (canned goods, peanut butter, or jelly) so that the quantities are easily seen. As each jar or can is used, the others slide to the front. When only one jar is visible, they know it's time to put the item on that week's grocery list. A kanban system is an easy way to visually check inventory levels and, according to lead times and other factors, place orders so that the item will be in stock as often as possible.

How can David and Heidi's 5S adventures help us understand the following:

- Identifying and removing *muda* during the 5S process?
- Standard work?
- Kanban?
- Kaizen and employee management?

Kanban cards (or other visual indicators) have been around for many years. In fact, what is called the "two-bin system" was used in the

United Kingdom long before Japanese manufacturing methodologies started to become popular in the 1970s. The two-bin system is discussed in greater detail in Chapter 13, "Brian's Lunch Dilemma." Whatever the origins, a kanban system is simple to visualize and easy to set up. Kanban systems are commonly used within the automotive industry. They are appropriate where there is a relatively stable demand and workflow.

The process starts when a specific amount of inventory is used, such as one boxful; when more of a product is needed, a signal (kanban card) is sent to a receiving area where all the supplies arrive. The card says what to order and what company you need to order it from: for example, a box of 100 cables from a company called Supplier. The card is put on a receiving board according to the date the new box is anticipated to arrive. When this box arrives, the card is taken from the receiving board and together with the box is delivered to the specified location, where it is stored.

This system is designed to be visual. All the same type of inventory is kept in one place. It should be easy to see how much of any part is on hand. For example, assume you start with three boxes of 100 cables. Each box has one card corresponding to it, for three cards in total. When one box is used, a signal (the kanban card) is sent to order another one. In the meantime, the second box is made available for use. When the parts in the second box are completely used, its kanban card is used to place another order. Before this second box is used up, a new box should have been delivered from Supplier. Rather than a complex computer system, the collection of kanbans and their placement on a kanban board provide a visual clue to inventory status and any late orders.

There are some "golden" rules for using the kanban system:

1. A kanban signal is issued only when a specific amount of the component it represents has been completely used up.
2. No kanban, no part. Items are ordered only when a kanban card exists.
3. No overproduction. Do not make or order any parts other than those that the kanban card asks for.
4. Components are manufactured only in the order the kanban cards are received, unless emergency kanbans are in use.

5. Components are ordered only in the amount specified by the kanban.
6. The number of kanban cards should be reduced over time, and the problems that are encountered in doing this should be tackled as they are exposed.
7. "Get to the gemba." To understand what is happening, go to the shop floor.

BRAIN PLAY

1. What suggestions do you have for David and Heidi to sustain their 5S home organization projects?
2. How could a dry-cleaning establishment improve its functional space using 5S?
3. Think about a situation in your personal or professional life where the use of 5S would be appropriate. Briefly describe the implementation steps.

PART III

Control

CHAPTER 10

Using Process Behavior Charts

TRACY SCOTT MANAGES HIS BLOOD SUGAR

As you eat and drink, glucose enters your bloodstream. Then your pancreas secretes a hormone that allows your body's cells to convert the glucose to energy—unless your pancreas doesn't. If that hormone doesn't materialize, the glucose will just sit there, and then you'll be in trouble.

Tracy Scott's pancreas didn't secrete that hormone. So several times a day, he had to determine his glucose level and whether he needed to inject the hormone—insulin—directly into his bloodstream with a needle. Such is the life of a person with type I diabetes. And food wasn't the only thing to consider: exercise, stress, health, environmental factors, and other

While enjoying lunch with his friend Daniel, Tracy, a diabetic, describes his plan to control his blood sugar levels. He distinguishes between routine variability and special, or assignable, causes (i.e., travel), which might require him to eat unfamiliar or nonoptimal foods. His close, systematic observation of the factors that might increase his blood sugar swings and his efforts to eliminate them have had the effect of establishing a continuous process for improving his self-care.

As you read Tracy's story, think about what he might do next on his path of continually improving his health.

medications could all affect glucose level. When it was high, Tracy added insulin, but when it was low, all he could do was ingest some carbohydrates as soon as possible, much as a blood donor is quickly offered juice and crackers.

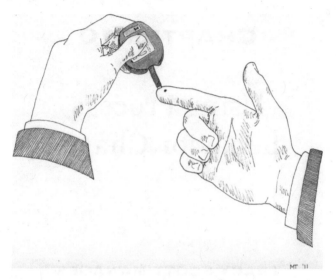

By planning his intake of carbohydrates at each meal, measuring his blood glucose level several times a day, and adjusting his insulin level by injection as needed, Tracy could avoid cardiovascular disease, kidney failure, nerve damage, blindness, and amputation, among other health risks. But keeping track of all this could be quite a complex process. Tracy had made a game of it—something he not only had to do but also was interested in doing. He used a spreadsheet to keep track of everything, for example, which gave him another excuse to carry around his tablet.

While out to lunch with a colleague, Daniel Stagnaro, Tracy recorded the hamburger and fries he ordered, piquing Daniel's curiosity.

MT '11

Daniel: What are you doing?

Tracy: I have diabetes. I use this spreadsheet to keep track of things that affect my blood sugar.

Daniel: Are you supposed to eat hamburgers?

Tracy: It's hard to know what to eat sometimes. There are so many factors that can affect your blood sugar when your body can't regulate it for you. Hamburgers are actually fine for my blood sugar; it's the fries I need to worry about.

Daniel: Really? Hamburgers?

Tracy: Hamburgers aren't the greatest in terms of fat content, but from a carb perspective, they're okay.

Daniel: I have to take cholesterol-lowering medication. I know the feeling. I don't like the idea that I need to take medication to stay healthy. Especially when the medication has other side effects.

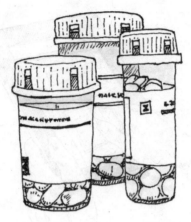

MT '11

Tracy: I have to take statins, too. On that front, the hamburger might not have been such a good idea. As a matter of fact, I take four medications related to the diabetes and cholesterol problem.

Daniel: I feel your pain.

Tracy: Well, we all get dealt a different hand of cards, right? I've got great children, an amazing wife, I love my job—not many people can say all that. Diabetes management is a pain, but it can be done. I use this spreadsheet to make a game of it.

Daniel: A game? How do you win?

Tracy: Every time I improve my process for managing the blood sugar variations and lowering the average level.

Daniel: What do you mean?

Tracy: It's just like any complex system with multiple, interacting inputs and one resulting measured output. In this case, the inputs to my spreadsheet are diet, exercise, medication, and special causes. Special causes are usually something environmental that's either outside of my control or a change from the normal routine. For instance, I usually bring my lunch. Today is different because I ordered off a menu. The output is my blood sugar, which I measure with this meter [*takes it out of his briefcase*] and these test strips.

Daniel: Hmm, I'm still not seeing the "game" here. It's great that you've got a system down, but I don't understand how you can improve.

Tracy: What I try to do is reduce my variability. Every time I notice something about my daily routine or habits that I could change to
improve this system of interacting factors, I make the change.
Then, if my variability goes down, I've won something.

Daniel: I'm starting to get it now. Tell me more.

Tracy: There are a few rules I've made up for myself over time. For
instance, a certain amount of output variation within a range
is nothing to worry about. It's just "noise" from normal stuff
at work in my body and in my daily routine. Some call these
common causes, such as the time of day or whether I'm at
work or at home. My blood sugar at the beginning of the day
is probably going to be different from how it is at the end. It's
just routine variation. Same with activity level. But it's not
anything I need to worry about, because it's variation within
an understandable range.

Daniel: But isn't eating fries a part of a normally varied life? Why would
you need to record that as a "special cause"?

Tracy: I didn't. I recorded it in the dietary column because right now
I'm focusing specifically on reducing fluctuation based on
menu choices. But normally I wouldn't note any food con-
sumption within a general range. It would be too hard to
analyze or take action on the data I'm collecting—too many
variables, if you factor in exercise and insulin amount.

Daniel: What other rules have you discovered?

Tracy: It's interesting, actually. Variation outside of this routine range
is almost always from a special cause—the trick is to figure
out what that cause is.

Daniel: How do you do that?

Tracy: Sometimes there's a pattern. If I've been on vacation and have
been eating in restaurants every night, or if I'm working out
of town and don't get enough sleep or exercise, or the local
diet is entirely different. Sometimes there's a single event I
can identify, such as a medication change. But sometimes
I can't figure it out at all.

Daniel: That would drive me crazy.

Tracy: Oh, yeah, you can go nuts trying to identify every little special
cause or trigger. So it's best to start with the obvious "assignable causes" of unacceptable variation, the kind that requires
additional insulin.

Daniel: So that's how you define a defect? A blood sugar level requiring more than the typical amount of insulin?

Tracy: Yes.

Daniel: And you win by removing the special causes of unacceptable variation?

Tracy: I win that way, and I also win by reducing the range of routine variation.

Daniel: How do you do that?

Tracy: Structural changes can cause the range to shrink or expand. These could be changes within my control or not. For instance, if I'm working in the home office, I can exercise 5 days a week. If this becomes a regular habit, then the routine variation in my blood sugar will be reduced. Which office I'm working from isn't in my direct control, but whether or not I exercise is.

Daniel: So if you're starting with a system that varies a lot, you'll want to cut down on special causes and make changes that cut down on the variability.

Tracy: That's right! The game part happens when you look at the data and make sense of it: which source of variation you should tackle first and why.

MT '11

Daniel: I suppose it helps you feel like you have more control over the condition. I don't know how well I'd do with that.

Tracy: It's not so bad. Like I said, I have so many other great things in my life that this hardly seems like a chore anymore. Actually, it's not just a feeling of having more control—I actually *have* more control. It's slow sometimes and can get frustrating, but I've seen consistent improvement since I started doing this.

Daniel: I'm impressed. So, how were your fries?

Tracy: Great! And well within my routine range of noise, so I can enjoy them in peace, without those nagging voices!

Daniel: Nonpunitive fries. The best kind.

HEALTH MANAGEMENT THROUGH PROCESS BEHAVIOR CHARTS

XmR CHARTS

Process behavior charts, also known as XmR charts, plot observations over time. XmR stands for *individual* (X) and *moving range* (mR). XmR charts consist of a single type of measurement—in this case, blood sugar—plotted over time. Often, the measurements occur in the context of many interacting variables that are difficult to separate.

In any process, the outputs are going to vary slightly. For example, blood sugar readings may vary throughout the day due to a number of factors. Some of this variability might be random, but occurs within a minimum and maximum range of expected variability. Some of the variability might be *because* of something.

Lean Takeaways

In a Lean implementation, part of the improvement process is the separation of "signal from noise"—which requires the use of simple statistical analysis tools to reduce variability.

Process behavior charts allow the observant user to distinguish between predictable and unpredictable variation. Predictable causes are referred to as "noise," whereas unpredictable causes are referred to as "special" or "assignable." Special causes offer the most fruitful lines of inquiry into improving a process and reducing variability, and noise can be safely ignored.

The next story, in Chapter 11, presents an approach to managing variability through a series of controlled experiments.

The purpose of an XmR chart is to try to tell these two types of variability apart: expected variability and variability due to a special or assignable cause. Variability due to a special cause might occur in the form of a pattern, such as too many data points in a row either above or below the average, or an alternating up-down arrangement.

Tracy Scott uses an XmR chart to observe his blood sugar and attempt to improve its stability. First, he attempts to recognize and separate this routine variability from "special" or assignable causes. Next, he takes steps to eliminate or reduce the assignable causes of variability. Last, he makes improvements that he believes will reduce the range of variability that he currently considers to be routine—lowering the maximum limit and raising the minimum limit. He initially targets those activities that he believes will benefit him the most.

SPECIAL AND ASSIGNABLE CAUSES

Once Tracy gets enough data on his XmR chart, he can begin to define the range of his routine variability with maximum and minimum limits. Routine variability in his blood sugar readings are scattered around the mean within these limits. Any variability above or below this range is due to a special cause, which he can try to eliminate or can choose to ignore. Sometimes a special cause of variability, such as "eating while traveling," can be prevented, prepared for, or predicted. If a special cause can be prevented, prepared for, or predicted, it might be worth addressing; if not, it might be better to ignore it.

The XmR limits define the current standard range, and not the range that Tracy wishes his blood sugar readings fell between. This standard range is referred to as the *voice of the process* (VOP). Creating a record of the outputs of a process can allow the process to "speak" and be recognized. Tracy's *desired* outcome for the process might be called the *voice of the customer* (VOC).

Sometimes, the stability of a process can be improved so it is less susceptible to the special cause. For example, someone in the process of losing weight might spend time building good eating and exercise habits. Then, a single large Thanksgiving meal may not result in an unacceptably high weight measurement. In another example, being able to more accurately predict a hurricane could help prevent loss or damage. When you know a hurricane is coming, it's a whole lot easier to board up the windows and wait in the cellar than it is to be caught unawares. Someone might learn from experience and prevent a special cause from affecting results by addressing underlying conditions before they become an issue.

Over time, taking steps to reduce the impact of special causes can create value by reducing variability. However, some special causes are simply beyond the control of the observer. We may be able to predict a giant meteor en route to New York City, but we could never prepare for or prevent the impact it might have. Business processes are the same way—some events are too big to predict, prevent, or prepare for. In these cases, investing resources into reducing one or more of the factors of routine variation might be more productive than addressing a special cause.

Tracy identifies travel as a root cause of some special variations. When he travels, he eats out more often out of necessity, which tends to throw his blood sugar readings off. He also tends to exercise less, but this is something he *can* control—everyone can do calisthenics in their hotel room, for example, or take a walk. Tracy must make decisions about the resources required to address any of the special causes he has identified and the order in which he should tackle them. Which are beyond his control? Which are easily controlled, and which are controllable with an investment? Which require simple behavior changes, for instance, and which require additional equipment or training? Answering these questions might help Tracy prioritize.

REDUCING VARIATION

Tracy's ultimate goal is to gain more control over the variability of his blood sugar readings by reducing the upper and lower limits of his routine variation, or the expected distribution of process output measurements around a mean. The XmR chart and the separation of output points into the categories of "special" and "routine" are just the first step.

Variability, whether special or routine, can be categorized in many ways, such as

- Internal or external
- Controllable or uncontrollable, given current circumstances
- Acceptable or unacceptable
- Preventable or unpreventable
- Predictable or not predictable
- Expensive or inexpensive to address

- Complex or simple
- Likely or unlikely to repeat or unlikely to repeat
- High or negligible impact on business or negligible impact on business

This list might help a manager assess causes of routine variation and prioritize improvement efforts. As improvements accumulate, the maximum and minimum limits that currently define the range of routine variability can be lowered and raised, respectively. When this happens, the data are scattered closer to the mean. This is a "new" routine range with lower process variation.

Continuous Improvement

Tracy slowly begins to reduce the range of what he considers to be routine variation. Over time, his work to control various contributing factors has become a "game" to him that he plays to win—so that he can minimize his insulin needs over his lifetime and reduce his potential risk. Every time he finds another creative way to limit his blood sugar fluctuations, he has won.

What insights can we gain from Tracy and Daniel's conversation over lunch that can help us understand the following:

- Process behavior charts?
- Special or assignable causes?
- Reducing variation?
- Continuous improvement?

In the preceding chapters, we discussed the collaborative spirit of kaizen as being an important part of the process. The cultural benefits of enthusiasm and personal commitment often represent the difference between an exciting, alive business and one that merely treads water. The fact that Tracy has made a game of reducing his blood sugar variability shows his commitment and positive attitude toward change and toward improving the process. Even though at first glance Tracy is undertaking this effort alone, he is actually doing it along with his family, doctor, and coworkers. For Tracy, this is an ongoing process that he will need to engage with for his entire life. Continuous improvement is also always a part of doing business, just as it is part of "doing life."

BRAIN PLAY

1. How else might Tracy improve his health through the use of process behavior charts?
2. How could a university's admissions office utilize process behavior charts? What metrics might be most useful to track and control in order to measure and increase effectiveness?
3. Think about a situation in your personal or professional life where the use of process behavior charts would be appropriate. Briefly describe what metrics you selected and what you would expect to see. What action items might be possible?

CHAPTER 11

Designing Experiments

BOB'S A-MAIZE-ING POPCORN

Bob: Hi, Jay. Thanks for making it over.

Jay: Glad to be here. Who else is here already? The game should be starting soon.

Bob: Mike and Dave are in the den, watching the pregame show and finalizing their fantasy teams. I think we've got about 15 minutes before kickoff.

Jay: Sounds good. Hey, what's that smell? Is something burning?

Bob [*runs to the kitchen*]: Whoops! I thought the guys were watching the stuff they brought. [*Frantically pulls on some oven mitts and slides out a tray of burned mozzarella sticks and chicken wings.*] Open the window!

Jay [*pops open a window and fiddles with the remote control for the ceiling fan*]: That's a lot of smoke.

Bob Leibe describes his son's science fair project—popping the perfect corn—to his friend, Jay, who has come over to watch a football game. He describes their process for identifying variables, as well as their objectives and definition of success. Last, he discusses the results of their research, which include insight into which variables have the greatest effect on the outcome.

As you read Bob's story, think about what he and his son might do next to continue the popcorn improvement process.

119

Bob: Give me that. [*Reaches for the remote control and puts the fan on high speed.*] Well, what are we going to eat now? Beer alone isn't enough. I've got to eat something, or my ulcer will act up.

Jay: I don't think anyone's going to want to go to the store again. What do you have in the house? Can we make some popcorn or something?

Bob: Good idea. [*Closes the window now that the smoke has cleared.*] I make the best popcorn this side of the Mississippi.

Jay: How could you possibly know that your popcorn is the best?

Bob: Because Malachi and I have popped a batch every day for the past month as part of his science project. For some reason, I haven't gotten tired of eating our research.

Jay: What's the science project about? I've got to do something similar with Vicky next month, and I could use some ideas.

Bob [gets his popcorn equipment out and opens a cabinet to reveal 12 bags of popcorn from different manufacturers]: We designed the project to demonstrate how to control several variables in a process to standardize and optimize the outcome.

Jay: What does Sandy have to say about all this?

Bob: She loves it. We always clean up the kitchen after conducting our top-secret activities. I usually cooked dinner anyway before we started this project because she worked late, and then she did the dishes—now it's easier for her because she gets dinner *and* a clean kitchen.

Jay: You're a real treasure!

Bob: Yeah, tell me about it. Anyway, we started the project by taking a look at the variables that we guessed would have the greatest effect on the outcome. We first looked at six variables, and we went back and forth about which ones were the most important. We wanted to design the project in the way we thought it would be most effective. When we first started talking about it, we looked at the brand of kernel, the thickness and density of the pan bottom, lid seal tightness, popping medium (oil or air), gas or electric stove, and toppings.

Jay: How would you even know where to start? That's not a very specific list. You could test those things forever and not come up with anything definitive. Don't science experiments isolate one or two things, so the outcome is more controlled?

Bob: Yes, that's true, but Malachi enjoys debating the minutiae, so we delved quite deeply into the details of those six things on our initial list. First of all, we have an electric stove, not a gas range. So we thought about that. We realized that our gas-versus-electric line item was more a matter of the ability to control temperature. For the purposes of this experiment, we realized that we could simply preheat an electric stove burner so that the popcorn pan was introduced to high heat fairly quickly, the same way as a gas stove. We also lowered the heat inside the popcorn pan by moving it to another burner that was not currently in use to duplicate the superior temperature control of a gas stove. Therefore, for the purposes of this experiment, we removed that variable from the list.

Instead, we focused on what we thought was the most effective temperature.

Jay: I think I follow you. What did you find?

Bob: We discovered that it didn't matter how long it took the burner to heat up, so long as it reached a high temperature. We learned we needed to create an environment of high pressure and high heat. By heating the burner sufficiently and making sure the lid was tight enough on the pan, we created the ideal conditions for popping corn. We also noted that control over the heat and pressure and the ability to adjust these conditions quickly were important. For instance, if we began to smell the popcorn burn or heard the popping rate slow down, we knew we needed to remove the pan from the heat source quickly to avoid burning.

Jay: You mean like how we just burned all the cheese sticks and chicken wings?

Bob: Exactly.

Jay: Did you rule out any of the other variables you mentioned in your initial list of six?

Bob: Well, we threw out the oil-or-air debate because we don't like air-popped popcorn.

Jay: I noticed that microwaves weren't in that list at all. Guess you don't like packaged microwave popcorn either?

Bob: You got it. That fake butter just doesn't do it for me.

Jay: So you made the choice to limit the experiment to oil-popped corn made on an unspecified stove.

Bob: You could say that, but we did end up listing butter, canola oil, and olive oil as three separate types of oil that we wanted to use as variables. So that line item changed.

Jay: That makes sense. What were you controlling the variables for— the best taste, or the least mess?

Bob: The best taste. Who cares about mess? That's immaterial if you've
   got a big bowl of fantastic popcorn in front of you.

Jay: Okay, so you weren't controlling for cleanliness as an outcome
   per se. But I'm sure you wanted to eliminate some form of
   waste in your process.

Bob: The waste elimination outcome we controlled for was "materials
   utilization"—the popcorn kernels. This scale had a low end
   and a high end, and our goal was to reduce variability within
   that range. We wanted all the kernels to be popped when we
   opened the pot, but we didn't want any to be popped and
   then burned. Too hot or too long on the heat source, and we
   would have had burned popcorn. Too cool, or not enough
   time on the heat source, and we would have unpopped kernels. So it was both of these extremes—the low end and the
   high end—that we controlled for in our quest to eliminate
   waste. I mean, really, what's more depressing than burned
   popcorn or tons of inedible kernels in your bowl? No one
   wants to break a tooth.

Jay: So what other rational decision did you arrive at in regard to your list of potential control variables? Gas versus electric was tossed out, and the popping mediums evolved based somewhat on your taste. Your experiment attempted to control the variables that optimized taste and reduced waste. What did the toppings have to do with anything?

Bob: You can come up with an infinite number of toppings, that's for sure. But since one of our objectives was to make the best-tasting popcorn based on our requirements, we decided that taste involved a topping or flavoring. We limited the toppings that we used in our research to three: plain salt, cheese-flavored popcorn salt, and sea salt with white truffle oil.

Jay: I read an article on truffle oil and popcorn a few months ago. Who knew?

Bob: I think it's the best thing since sliced bread. Malachi didn't care for it much, though, and his taste was part of the experiment. We found that the cheese-flavored salt had an aftertaste. After all was said and done, we both liked plain salt the best. Once we narrowed it down to plain salt, we determined that the coarse-ground salt was the best. So the toppings variable was a self-limiting experiment that wasn't dependent on multiple variables the way the actual popping process was. That process involved everything: heat and pressure, the ability to react quickly and change conditions when necessary, and tightness of the pan lid seal and density of the pan bottom.

Jay: I'll say it again—that's a lot of variables to control.

Bob: Well, we tried a couple of different pans, and figured out that the cast iron or enamel-coated pans work best—when the seal from the matching lid is tight enough. We were able to control those conditions easily. The variables that were more complicated were those that required judgment and careful monitoring. You really have to know what you're doing to make popcorn.

Jay: So isn't that another variable, then—the skill and experience of the chef? Maybe part of the reason you're so good at making popcorn now is simply because you've paid so much attention to the places where you need to make split-second decisions. Could it be that it's merely your experience making popcorn that makes it so much better, and it's nothing to do with your control of the variables?

Bob: It's possible but unlikely. The nice thing about this science project, despite the fact that it's inexact and rather bumbling, is that we *have* taken some measurements along the way.

Jay: I still think that this is more along the lines of a practicum than a true experiment.

Bob: Well, it's true. We don't have precision equipment, and we didn't set up a complex computer algorithm to decipher the precise interaction of the various conditions and compare that to the resulting taste and utilization of the popcorn. But we've identified several variables that we considered would have a high impact on conditions, and we looked for ways to understand and quickly take action to improve or control those conditions based on experimentation—even if that experimentation was only a simple comparison, like choosing the best pan or the most flavorful topping. I like to say, "Don't let perfect get in the way of better!" The popping process itself was more complex, but we still improved our results significantly, and I don't think that's just because we were paying attention. I think we controlled the variables to influence the outcome, as well. Why don't you take a look at our spreadsheet? We have a computer in the den.

Jay: You mean the same room where the game is supposed to start in 30 seconds?

Bob: The very one.

Jay: Maybe that can be a halftime activity.

Bob: Perfect.

Jay: Hey, this is good popcorn!

USING EXPERIMENTS TO CREATE
THE BEST POPCORN

EXPERIMENTAL DESIGN

Bob and his son use the scientific method to design an experiment intended to answer a high-level question, "How do you pop the perfect popcorn?" They create a defined set of variables, form a hypothesis, and design a method for answering this question. Then, they analyze their findings and come to conclusions that help shape their future behavior.

A method is a set of activities intended to produce a set of outputs that will help the researcher answer a question. Ideally, the researcher will make adjustments based on the results. Sometimes, research results are available immediately; at other times, it can be many years before results are available. Regardless of the time frame, researchers are as specific as possible about the question, hypothesis, variables, method, analysis, and conclusions. Rigorous experimental methodology provides a roadmap to others so that experiments do not need to be duplicated in order to build upon the findings, yet they have the possibility of being duplicated if the findings need to be confirmed.

Lean Takeaways

The relationships between the inputs and outputs of a process aren't often clear, and Lean tools seek to help teams learn more about these relationships. A controlled experiment with well-defined variables can help discern what needs to be done next in order to better meet customer requirements. While controlled experiments are often associated with Six Sigma, they can also be helpful in a Lean application when used to improve an organization's understanding of its value stream and customer-needs fulfillment.

Once a process has been established, the next step is to ensure that the output of the process remains consistent. This is accomplished in part through total productive maintenance, which will be discussed in Chapter 12.

The experiment in this story was limited in nature. There were only a few defined variables, some with yes-or-no answers. Bob and Malachi were not really searching for the perfect popcorn. They were looking for answers to specific questions: what tastes better—olive oil, canola oil, or butter? What's the best topping: plain salt, sea salt with truffle oil, or cheese-flavored popcorn salt? What temperature and heat seal are least wasteful? Because their questions were more specific than simply "What's the best popcorn?" their experiment yielded more interesting results. Bob and Malachi also took the time to think about the variables that might contribute most to the final product.

Broadly, research is something that individuals and organizations do on a continual basis. The scientific method can be the basis for innovation because it is an effective way to compile and communicate results and to create a roadmap between where we *were* and where we *are*. The breadcrumbs of Hansel and Gretel are a mythological kind of roadmap—but in the story this path of crumbs is eaten by birds, and the children become lost. Research at its best is intentional, permanent, and duplicable. *Innovation*, that slippery word that implies creative sparks and genius twists of mental clarity, is at its core well-directed, well-documented, and well-applied research.

Six Sigma

Bob and his son attempt to control variability in the making of popcorn. They loosely use a sequence of Six Sigma steps, which are *Define*, *Measure*, *Analyze*, *Implement*, and *Control*, or *DMAIC*.

Six Sigma is typically used by organizations to improve a particular part of a process. It is often thought of as a longer-term, 6- to 12-month process that is geared toward a specific outcome—for example, reducing defects to fewer than three per million opportunities. The idea that a process can be controlled by limiting the spread of outcome measurements is related to the XmR charts described in Chapter 10. Six Sigma uses rigorous data collection to try to produce changes of statistical significance. The current state of what is considered to be "routine" distribution is tightened around the mean, and variability is reduced through a systematic means.

First, the process to be examined is *d*efined. Participants also define what they believe are the factors that cause the most variability, as well as the desired results. Next, the variables that have been identified as being most relevant are *m*easured and *a*nalyzed to determine which of those variables should be acted upon first. The *i*mplementation step requires changes to the process to reduce the variability or move the process closer toward a desired future state. Last—since the primary challenge for any individual or organization is usually maintaining a new state once it has been attained—the *c*ontrol phase includes measures taken to protect and preserve the improvements to the process.

Depending on how important the process is to the value proposition, sometimes the DMAIC is a cycle that continues. For Tracy Scott in Chapter 10, reducing his blood sugar variability is an activity that he will be engaged in for his lifetime. For some companies, continually improving the taste of a product will be an ongoing endeavor. For other, large companies, Six Sigma projects are constantly being proposed throughout the entire organization. Return on investment (ROI) estimations are submitted with these proposals and help determine which projects are funded and staffed. Full-time Master Black Belts and significant staff training are all part of the expense associated with a Six Sigma project, which typically lasts around 6 months. The ROI that is associated with the statistically significant improvement to a process, therefore, must be competitive with regard to the entire pool of project proposals.

Six Sigma projects typically represent a deep-dive exploration into a particular process. Leaders should understand where, when, how, and under what circumstances to undertake such a study. Those projects that are most closely related to the organization's ability to deliver its value proposition are typically most important.

How can Bob and his son's experiments with perfect popcorn help us understand more about the following:

- Experimental design?
- Six Sigma?
- Designing a robust process?
- Accuracy versus precision?
- Defining and limiting variables?

DESIGNING A ROBUST PROCESS

A robust process is one that is less susceptible to the potential negative effects of some force—a force that might affect the ability of the process to produce a desirable output. For instance, consider a cookie-baking machine. The machine itself is old and has problems regulating its internal temperature. The cookies are often either burnt or undercooked. A business manager has two choices: either spend money to fix the machine, or formulate a new cookie dough that produces a more consistent cookie regardless of the variability in cooking temperature. Formulating new cookie dough is an example of improving the internal robustness of a process. Cookies made with the new cookie dough come out great, regardless of fluctuations in cooking temperature.

People can also make their own processes more robust. One example is the practice of meditation. Meditation encourages individuals to notice environmental distractions or disruptions, and to make the choice not to react. In essence, the practice of meditation helps individuals to make their own mental process *more robust* by training the mind to be less reactive to environmental triggers. What was once perceived as a distraction might no longer be a distraction; therefore, the mental process is more robust even when no changes were made to the external environment.

Another example is the management of an allergy condition. An allergy sufferer has two choices: avoid situations that might present allergy triggers (external), or take steps to limit the reactivity of their immune system (internal). This might include symptomatic approaches such as medication or some other treatment, such as allergy shots, intended to reduce the reactivity of the system. This is an example of making a process more robust.

Bob and his son attempt to make their process more robust by considering the likely variability of their heat source and the burnt popcorn that might result. They account for this heat variability by heating up the burner first, and moving the pan around on the burner while it is being heated. They add extra oil so the kernels are more evenly coated. This approach is distinct from a special- or assignable-causes management approach where the offending root cause of the process disruption (i.e., the variability in the heat source) is addressed. In this case, Bob and his son respond to the variability by adjusting the process, so the process itself is more capable of tolerating variability.

ACCURACY VERSUS PRECISION

An electric stove might be either precisely the wrong temperature or accurate (on average) in terms of the average temperature but with high variability. For this reason, Bob and his son prefer the gas stove, because they think that they can "eyeball" the temperature more accurately. They also prefer the gas stove because they believe that they can change the temperature more quickly when necessary to optimize the popping process. Since they have an electric stove, they invent ways to achieve similar results by heating the electric burner in advance and moving the pan to another, unheated burner when necessary to prevent burning.

In a business context, this distinction is important because settings on machines are susceptible to process issues of their own. It is important to be able to discern the difference between accuracy and precision. Any process that is dependent on readings of any kind—such as temperature readings on ovens, or oil check levels on packaging equipment—can be negatively affected. "Inaccurate, yet precise" means being off all the time to the exact same degree. One example of this is a clock that is set 5 minutes fast. "Imprecise, yet accurate" means high variability that is accurately measured, on average. An example is a flashlight that flickers, measured by a light meter that tells you exactly how much light is being produced.

DEFINING AND LIMITING VARIABLES

Bob and his son spend a good deal of their experimental design time on the identification of variables. They brainstorm a list and then categorize and consolidate based on a number of factors. Taking a leadership perspective is important when defining and limiting variables, because linking these variables to broader goals is what makes any research project meaningful. The links between variables, overall experimental design, and broader goals are especially important when research is undertaken with a longer time horizon.

For instance, individuals conduct "research" about life all the time. They begin with a question: "Is this the right career path?" "Is this the right relationship?" or "Should I invest resources into social media marketing for my company?" When people design experiments that explore certain questions about life or business, the variables they choose might yield the most fruitful information when those variables link back to deeply held beliefs, for instance, or a desired future state.

BRAIN PLAY

1. What other experiments could Bob and his son conduct next to accomplish their goal of perfect popcorn?
2. How could a credit card company create new financial products using the experimental design concepts?
3. Think about a situation in your personal or professional life where conducting a set of experiments would be appropriate. What performance metrics would you use, and what variables would you evaluate?

CHAPTER 12

Maintaining Reliable Equipment

MISSY'S CAR MAINTENANCE

Recent MBA grads Kate Horner and Missy Gillespie rented condos in the same building in Adams Morgan, near downtown Washington, DC. Both were new to the area, having rented their condos immediately after graduating from business school. They met while walking to the same Bikram yoga class a few blocks away.

The condo was a popular place to live due to its proximity to the Metro station and the zoo, as well as its covered parking garage. Missy usually took the subway to work, but she would drive if she had errands or knew she would be arriving home late.

Missy Gillespie thinks critically about her systems for maintaining her vehicle—starting with her choice to lease or buy a new or used car. She talks with her friend about the ways in which she monitors her vehicle for problems, plans her service visits, and tries to control the effects of unpredictable events.

As you read Missy's story, think about the choices she made when purchasing her car and how they affect her approach to maintenance.

Shortly after moving, Missy began to notice certain things going wrong with her classic luxury sedan which she had bought used from her uncle 3 years earlier. She shared her frustrations with Kate one day over coffee and biscotti at a neighborhood café.

Missy: So I took my car to a mechanic last week because the seat was all whacked out, right? And when I go to pick it up, he hadn't done anything.

Kate: Whacked out how?

Missy: It's a power seat, only every now and then it moves by itself, and when I stop quickly at a red light it comes forward. I'm not sure why this happens. It used to be my uncle's, and he's kind of large; he could have messed it up.

Kate: Sure.

Missy: The guy said he couldn't repeat the problem.

Kate: Of course.

Missy: He said the servo was fine. But when I take it for a ride, the seat still moves, and then I start to hear a noise I hadn't heard before, and he said he couldn't find anything wrong and that maybe my boyfriend would have better luck.

Kate: Jerk.

Missy: It was pretty shocking, really. I should know if something's wrong with it, right? I'll be trying a new place—one that takes women seriously.

Kate: It's kind of like DuPont.

Missy: Dupont Circle?

Kate often took a philosophical approach to life. An industrial engineering major undergrad who focused on operations in her MBA program, she had become a Lean and Six Sigma process improvement consultant, and she tended to relate everyday happenings to an operations framework. She found that doing so improved both her personal life and professional capability, since everyday examples helped her communicate better with her clients.

Kate: I'm sorry—DuPont the company. I mean how well people know and maintain equipment when they feel like they own it. What you just told me, other than being an example of jerkdom, is also an example of you having better knowledge about your car because you drive it all the time and your having the necessary time to fix it because you have a vested interest in taking care of it.

Missy: Okay ...

Kate: When you fill up your own car with gas, what kind of gas do you use?

Missy: The car recommends high-octane, like a 93. It's expensive, but I don't drive it that much and I'd hate to have a problem with the engine.

Kate: What kind of gas do you put in a rental car?

Missy: I put in the cheapest stuff I can find, of course. And when I run over a pothole, I'm like, "Sure am glad this isn't my car!" [*They laugh.*]

Kate: Manufacturers using large equipment have that same feeling of ownership. You're going to take care of a machine differently depending on how you feel about it, right?

Missy: Probably.

Kate: I've heard that DuPont actually labels its machines with the names of its operators. They engage the employees so each operator has the feeling that he or she actually owns the equipment, and as a result—this is what they say—maintenance costs, downtime, and reliability statistics are much better.

Missy: You are a fountain of knowledge. So I still have a broken seat, but it's like part of the family. [*The women laugh and then chew thoughtfully on their biscotti.*] I really like having my own parking space. It makes it easy to check for oil leaks, monitor the air conditioning drips, that sort of thing.

Kate: Like the DuPont example, there's less contamination. It's a controlled environment, so it's easier to isolate and detect problems. It reduces the number of variables. There's something to be said for consistency, that's for sure. I'm just happy I *have* a parking space. I like that it's protected.

Missy: True. It's definitely a bonus for these condos.

Kate: How much do you have to take care of your car, anyway? I barely have to do anything to my Camry. I leased it brand new last year. I just take it in when I need the oil changed. It doesn't need a whole lot.

Missy: Mine is a 1995. I have to check the fluids and keep them topped off. Especially when I'm about to drive home for the holidays or go on a trip, I make sure to give everything a once-over. I've learned how to check those things with this car. But I love my old antique. It's worth knowing the little tricks and what to watch out for to keep her running.

Kate: Completely. I get it. [*She takes a sip of coffee.*] Well you know, that just goes right back to what I was saying about DuPont. You're the operator of that vehicle, and you do the maintenance and repairs. Therefore, you're more personally invested in that machine's successful operation and preventive maintenance.

Missy: Well, aren't you invested in your beautiful, spanking-clean Camry, too?

Kate: Not in the same way. I just expect my car to work when I get in it and push the "on" button. That's why I lease, because I don't *want* to be invested. I just want the thing to work.

Missy: Hmmm. Interesting. But your car is going to get old someday too, and the time you put into it now will pay off later. You still have to pay for your own repairs when it's leased, right?

Kate: Yes you do, and you're right. But I have to consider what it's worth to me to reduce my uncertainty. Once this lease is over, I'm probably going to trade it in and lease another new car. It's like any other capital expenditure: There's a tipping point where the maintenance required to keep a machine running and the technological potential of that machine just don't add up. You can either make a calculated investment in something new—which may take 1, 2, maybe 5 years to pay off and then it needs to be replaced again—or just live with the fact that you're probably going to need to make unscheduled repairs at some point, usually when you least expect it.

Missy: Well, that's the deal with the preventive maintenance I'm talking about. I love my old car, and when I pay attention to certain aspects of its proper functioning that I can control, in effect I *do* reduce my uncertainty—because some potential problems are avoidable. And when they're avoided, then so is the whole repair process: breaking down on the road, waiting for parts to be delivered, time off from work, the extra money, the hassle, the whole deal.

Kate: And don't forget about predictive maintenance.

Missy: What's that?

Kate: One of the best things about my cars is that they have always worked. Every morning, I have been able to get up, start my car, and make it to work safely. That doesn't come cheap. Like they say, "Good maintenance costs money. Poor maintenance costs even more." Although I pay for the maintenance, many problems are prevented, and repairs are made correctly the first time since the mechanics are well trained. I can also forget about the inconveniences of a car breakdown, the costs of a towing or repair service, and the additional wait for spare parts. My car maintenance program involves two important aspects. There are the planned maintenance activities, such as the oil changes, and the 10,000-mile service. In addition, there are the predictive maintenance activities, such as refilling the gas tank when the red indicator light comes on, and scheduling service when other warning indicators tell me there are potential problems. Of course, there may be some reactive maintenance activities, like a flat tire created by going over a nail at a construction site. But all in all, I really believe that I can maintain my car so that I can essentially eliminate failures.

Missy: That's fine for you, but what gets in the way of a company performing those tasks well?

Kate: Like anything else, the primary driver of a deficit in maintenance—preventive or predictive—is lack of money. But I believe that it's also a matter of the sense of ownership that operators have about their tools. And building engagement is a matter of leadership and the cultural norms of the company, not something that happens by itself. Which brings me back to your car.

Missy: It's true. I love my car, and I know it so well that I think I can avoid unplanned maintenance—downtime—almost completely.

Kate: All that's left is for you to put a label with your name on it.

Missy: Ha! And mud flaps that say, "Back off!"

IMPROVING AUTOMOBILE PERFORMANCE THROUGH TOTAL PRODUCTIVE MAINTENANCE

PREDICTIVE, PREVENTIVE, AND REACTIVE MAINTENANCE

The predictive-preventive-reactive triad defines three approaches to equipment maintenance:

- *Reactive approaches* mean that if something's not broken, it doesn't get fixed.
- *Preventive approaches* use scheduled repairs at predetermined intervals, regardless of apparent need. Examples of this are the 3,000-mile oil change, aircraft engine overhauls, and medical checkups.

Lean Takeaways

Planned equipment maintenance is an essential part of total productive maintenance, because it reduces the likelihood of unexpected downtime overall. Making time in advance to think through a context-specific equipment maintenance plan helps ensure that a process remains as consistent and reliable as possible—and consistency and reliability are basic tenets of Lean.

This chapter concludes the section on control, and now we move into the fourth "C," coordination. We have completed the internal improvement process, we will expand our view outside the organization to work with suppliers.

- *Predictive approaches* use indicators for repair such as a check engine light, blood pressure measurement, or cholesterol check.

In practice, things usually aren't so simple—business and life change so rapidly that a combination approach is usually warranted. Not everything can be maintained perfectly. This is especially true if perfect maintenance has a negative impact on an organization's ability to deliver its value proposition, or if needed resources won't be available for other more critical opportunities. It helps tremendously to categorize repair efforts into one of these three strategies. A more robust maintenance process makes greater use of preventive and predictive strategies and minimizes instances of reactivity. Reactive maintenance strategies tend to result in less robust processes that are more susceptible to delay and unforeseen expense.

Because a combination approach is generally the most feasible, there is not often one easy answer. Some equipment is best serviced at regular intervals, because the cost of purchasing, installing, maintaining, monitoring, and using the available predictive measurement tools is too high. Even if a predictive approach demonstrates a reduction in equipment downtime or failure, the predictive measurement tools may still be too expensive.

Missy and Kate make use of each of these approaches in varying ways. Kate leases a new car with the expectation that her maintenance investment will be minimal; she pays a monthly fee to minimize her risk of downtime. Vehicle maintenance is not fun for her, so she is willing to pay someone else. Missy, on the other hand, owns a classic car that is older and requires some creative investments in terms of time, skill, and finances to maintain—but she enjoys the process and is good at it. She accepts the risk of an older vehicle because it's a good fit for her capabilities and interests, and because she is able to contain that risk through a combined *predictive* and *preventive* strategy and her knowledge of her vehicle's mechanics. She *prevents* problems through scheduled maintenance such as checkups and oil changes, and she *predicts* by responding quickly to any indicator lights on her dash, like the fuel or check engine lights or a new rattling sound. She controls the environmental variability by parking her car in a covered lot, often in the same place. Because she limits the environmental "noise" that might cause problems with her vehicle, Missy can observe her vehicle over time for drips or spills, in a controlled setting. Controlling the setting is another *predictive* technique.

What can we learn from Missy and Kate's conversation about improving automobile performance through:

- Predictive, preventive, and reactive maintenance?
- Total productive maintenance?
- Supplier relationships?

The story also explores ownership of equipment when it mentions that DuPont affixes the names of machine operators to their respective machines. This practice, combined with an extensive continuous improvement initiative that involves, engages, educates, and empowers employees, has been correlated with significant downtime reduction for machines. The mix of *predictive*, *preventive*, and *reactive* strategies that is employed for a given piece of equipment should be determined by the degree of ownership felt by its operator.

SUPPLIER RELATIONSHIPS

Missy tells her friend that she did not have a good experience at the first garage to which she took her vehicle, and that she felt that her gender was a factor in how she was treated. This may or may not have been the case—but it was enough that Missy felt uncomfortable, and she went elsewhere because she had other options. Mutual trust and mutually agreeable expectations regarding how a transaction will take place and how both parties will gain value are parts of a productive professional environment.

Businesses sometimes abandon relationships with suppliers, partners, and distributors when things don't pass the "gut" test. Could better communication, however, have been a more valuable solution? Sometimes the most valuable relationship is the one that is already in place—and sometimes it's throwing good money after bad to continue to invest resources in a relationship that just doesn't feel right. A good leader can identify when it's time to go in a different direction—and uses that knowledge to make better choices in the future.

Luckily, Missy has other options. There are plenty of garages and mechanics that are willing to take her money in exchange for helping her maintain her vehicle. The law of supply and demand applies to some extent, because the availability of other options is a factor in her decision. This abundance of options or buying power isn't always the case, however. When the number of suppliers or other external stake-holders is more limited, then sometimes the only option is the current one. Trust and transparency are essential. Without trust, it's easy for a relationship to deteriorate over a few ill-chosen phrases.

BRAIN PLAY

1. What other applications of total-productive-maintenance thinking can Kate and Missy use to improve the productivity of their daily activities?
2. How could an executive-leadership coach encourage his or her clients to use the principles of total productive maintenance?
3. Think about a situation in your personal or professional life where the application of total-productive-maintenance thinking would be beneficial. Briefly describe each of the implementation steps.

PART IV

Coordination

CHAPTER 13

Designing a Supply Chain

BRIAN AND TONYA'S LUNCH DILEMMA

Brian and Tonya Venuti were constantly bickering about ways to put money aside for a vacation to Rome. For some reason, these discussions always seemed to involve the packing of lunches.

Brian and Tonya Venuti plan to save money by bringing their lunches from home—and to use the money they save to take a vacation to Rome. The couple examines their lunch habits and techniques for managing lunch fixings.

The two of them required 40 lunches each month. They calculated that sandwich-and-drink cart stops and sit-down lunch meetings averaged out to $15 each, whereas lunches brought from

As you read Brian and Tonya's story, think about what choices and trade-offs the couple makes when deciding on the appropriate lunch management system for their situation.

home averaged $5. The latter also tended to be both more nutritious and more conducive to weight control, a priority for both.

Theoretically, if they brought their lunches from home every day, they could put $400 a month into an escrow account for their Rome vacation, which over 12 months would net $4,800—enough for a nice 10-day stay.

Brian: Okay, if we're going to do this, I want to do it right. Let's not just make a lame attempt and fail miserably once again because we didn't think this through.

Tonya: What do you have in mind?

Brian: Well, my idea was to apply the concepts of inventory control that I've been learning in my business-school classes to the way we approach packing lunch, to see if we can keep enough stuff on hand to avoid running out.

Tonya: Well, not running out of lunch stuff would eliminate that issue, for sure. But the other barrier to bringing lunch every day is that sometimes we have lunch meetings. And sometimes, frankly, I just don't feel like bringing it.

Brian: I hear you. I know. Maybe we could plan on buying one lunch per week. It will eat into that nice $4,800 check, though.

Tonya: But honey, it's more realistic, and $3,840 is still a nice sum.

Brian: But can I tell you how I think we can improve the process?

Tonya: Go for it.

Brian: I've categorized the lunches we bring into "microwavable," "leftovers," and "freshly prepared." The leftovers are one thing we probably shouldn't count on. If we ever have enough for a nice lunch the next day, it's a bonus.

Tonya: That makes sense, since we usually eat leftovers for the next night's dinner anyway. And the "microwavable" option?

MT '11

Brian: Those are the easiest to keep in inventory and take with us but not quite as nutritious as something freshly made. I think the issue with those is in the amount purchased at a time, and the reorder point. We usually go food shopping once a week, right?

Tonya: Right...

Brian: So instead of just buying 5 or 6 at a time, and refilling the freezer when we're out, we can double the amount we get at the store to 10 or 12, and when we notice we only have 4 left, we can put it on the list.

Tonya: Brilliant, Sherlock. So one option is to double the order quantity and move up the restock point to four lunches, instead of zero. That way, we won't have to purchase items as frequently because we're buying more at one time. Also, by putting it on the list when we have four left, we'll be less likely to run out.

Brian: Precisely, Watson.

Tonya: So what about the freshly made lunch option?

MT '11

Brian: Fresh lunches are the hardest. You have to keep a lot of ingredients on hand that run out at different times: peanut butter and jelly, cold cuts, salads, tuna, bread, condiments, drinks, fruit—it's a lot to keep up with.

Tonya: Tell me about it. Alexa goes to three or four different grocery stores a week because Trevor will eat only beige food, Emily has to eat gluten-free, and then vegetables and meat for everybody because of that whole balanced-diet thing.

Brian: It's got to be hard for your sister to be alone most of the week with Jack on the road. I wish he were able to help her out more.

Tonya: Well, yeah. He does what he can. Maybe he'll consider a career change at some point, but with the economy the way it is, they are lucky that he has such a great job. Anyway, let's focus on our lunch plan. We're almost there. We just have to figure out what our restock system should be.

Brian: What goes stale the quickest is the fruit and bread. So maybe we should base our system using that as a standard.

Tonya: The more I think about it, the more I question whether having a fixed reorder point is the way to go in this case. I wonder if we should just make a weekend trip to the store and *always* stock up on a pre-established list of ingredients. We'd replace anything that was used throughout the week, whether it was a microwave lunch or a ham sandwich—so every Monday we start the week with the same quantity of stuff. That way we can get a little variety too. Instead of automatically restocking celery or apples, maybe we're in the mood for peaches that week.

Brian: I think you've got something. We could have categories, say fresh fruit, veggies, and deli meat, so we can stock up with any food that's on sale, or in season, or that suits our fancy that week.

Tonya: Suits our fancy, yes. Great expression. I picture a moonlit night in Rome, eating homemade pasta and drinking Chianti.

Brian: Well, one more thing before you drift off into the land of *Lady and the Tramp* sharing a pasta noodle: I think we should make our lunches the night before. [*He cringes, expecting her to object.*]

Tonya: No, you're probably right. It's not like we have kids. I suppose we could take time away from watching reruns to make lunch.

Brian: I'll do that to go to Rome.

Tonya: All lunches lead to Rome.

MANAGING THE SUPPLY CHAIN
FOR A HOME-COOKED LUNCH

There are competing objectives when managing inventories. *Marketing* would like to have enough finished goods inventory to always have products available for customers. *Finance* looks to minimize the investment in inventory. *Manufacturing* might like to have large batches of items (inventories) to save on setup or ordering costs. Because these objectives often conflict, operations managers must reconcile them when they pursue coordination policies that contribute to the overall success of the firm.

Brian and Tonya balance the costs of holding excessive lunch-ingredient-inventory against the cost of running out. Too much inventory results in spoilage and lost opportunities to deploy money elsewhere. Too little inventory results in a shortage cost—which takes the form of having to buy lunches instead of bringing them from home.

Lean Takeaways

While inventory is one of the seven classic forms of Lean-defined waste, it can also serve a purpose. In this case, Brian and Tonya were able to reduce the number of trips to the supermarket by batching purchases and holding inventory of food products. In this case, the supermarket is the couple's supplier—and the relationship between the buyer and supplier must be considered. For any purchase, there are transaction costs, holding costs, and costs of running out.

In the next chapter, we will study ordering and review systems in another context—as well as quantity discounts, life cycle costing, and visual management systems.

THE REORDER POINT SYSTEM

A reorder point system (ROP), sometimes called a continuous-review system, works almost like waves in the sea. A new order of some fixed amount is delivered; the item's inventory then dwindles gradually as it is used. No more of that item is ordered again until the water level has reached a low point. Then, a new wave comes in, and the inventory is replenished! The "wave" of inventory might recede at slightly different rates each time. The low-water line and the fixed order amount determine when to order and how much to order. The average number of orders per year is the total annual demand divided by the reorder quantity.

The ROP system requires the user to monitor inventory at all times and reorder when the supply reaches a certain point. This point should be chosen to allow for regular usage plus some safety stock. The safety stock should account for surges in demand as well as the length and variability of the lead time required to receive the new order.

The amount to order depends on a few factors. Sometimes, this amount is determined by past practice or by judgment. It can also be calculated using a formula that helps determine what is called the *economic order quantity*, or EOQ. We discuss the EOQ in greater detail in "Peter Goes Shopping" in Chapter 14. It is a fixed amount that typically does not change, except perhaps after an annual review. The new order arrives after a lead time elapses. Because of this waiting period, the amount needed between placing the order and the time the order arrives is also important. Typically, the reorder quantity is reevaluated each year based on demand, demand fluctuation, lead time, and other factors.

What do Brian and Tonya's goals to reduce the cost of lunch reveal about:

- Economic order quantity?
- Reorder point?
- Periodic or continuous review?
- Safety stock and cycle stock?

A kanban system is similar to a ROP system (often referred to as a *two-bin system*). A kanban card or some other visual cue is used to signal when the reorder point has been reached. The cue may be that the first bin is empty, and the second bin is being used. All demand is initially satisfied from the first bin. When the first bin is empty, the item is reordered. During the reorder lead time, items in the second bin are used to fill demand. Using this system, the amount of stock kept in the second bin equals the reorder point quantity.

When Brian and Tonya discuss the dynamics of their microwave lunch supply, they consider the ROP system but don't ultimately choose it. They abandon this initial plan in favor of a periodic review system, described below, that only requires them to check their freezer at a fixed weekly interval and to "order" new lunches then.

PERIODIC REVIEW SYSTEMS

While someone using an ROP system orders the same quantity each time the inventory levels of an item reaches a low-water mark—but the time between orders will vary—someone using a periodic review system (PR) will instead order *different* amounts of the item at *fixed* intervals. The image here is of a waitress that *always* wants your coffee cup full. She'll make her rounds of the restaurant, stopping at your table every 10 minutes, and fill your cup up to the top whether it's half-empty, almost completely empty, or just to top it off.

PR systems are most often used when there is an external reason for a repeating interval to be selected, such as weekly trips to the grocery, or when a supplier might visit once a month to refill inventories of many different products. The inventory level of an item is reviewed at regular (periodic) intervals and at that time, a decision is made on how much to order. The review period and the target inventory level determine when to order and how much to order of each item. In contrast to the ROP system, the time between orders is fixed but the amount ordered varies. Hence, this system is sometimes referred to as a fixed-period system. Another common name for the PR system is an order-up-to system because of the rule of ordering-up-to the target level each time a review is performed.

The target level is based on two things: the "cycle" stock that is expected to be used between order points, and the extra "safety" stock that might be required to accommodate changes in demand. These amounts can be determined through statistical or economic analysis or by judgment. Cycle stock and safety stock are covered in greater detail in "Brad and Gina and Baby Make Three" in Chapter 15.

The review period can be determined by convenience (e.g., review multiple items from a given category or supplier every 2 weeks), through internal administrative practices that have historically governed the procurement process, or through an economic analysis that trades off the cost of ordering against the cost of holding inventory. Brian and Tonya use a weekly review period for its simplicity and convenience, particularly on frequently ordered items that come from a few key suppliers—grocery stores.

Brian and Tonya ultimately choose a PR system for the management of their lunch supplies. They check their inventory at fixed weekly intervals when they look in the refrigerator and fill their order at that time during their weekend trip to the grocery store. They consider their overall goal, which is to have sufficient lunch ingredients to pack lunches 4 days a week without a stock-out, the freshness of the ingredients, the ease of preparation, and the variety of the lunches packed.

They compare the cost to acquire and the cost to hold when they discuss taking one trip to the store each weekend to buy fresh ingredients that are in season. They purchase fresh foods in categories such as deli meats, fruit, and dairy—and "order up to" a predetermined quantity for each category. At that time, since they're already at the store, they plan to refill items in the microwave-lunch category. Finally, they compare the potential benefits of holding extra inventory to the benefit of fresher, more varied ingredients and determine that the latter is more in line with their goals as a couple.

BRAIN PLAY

1. What else can Brian and Tonya do to minimize their lunch costs?
2. How should a convenience store manage supplier relations?
3. Think about a situation in your personal or professional life where reexamining a reorder point and introducing a periodic- or continuous-review system would be appropriate. Briefly describe each of the implementation steps.

CHAPTER 14

Determining Lot Size

PETER GOES SHOPPING

Peter Orville was an MBA for Executives student who was currently between roles. Previously, he had been an operations and logistics manager for a Dallas-based hardwood lumber, millwork, and flooring supplier. In this role, he had negotiated the procurement of a variety of resources. He enjoyed the process of establishing optimal reorder quantities as well as those aspects of his job that allowed him to establish and

Peter Orville examines his purchasing and inventory control systems with his neighbor, Paul. His objective is to even out his purchasing patterns by making smaller, more frequent purchases. They also discuss ways to monitor his progress.

As you read Peter's story, think about the trade-offs he has made. Has Peter's home been optimized by making these changes?

improve upon processes. His motto while on the job was always that of a gemba walk[1] proponent: "Go and see," he'd say. He believed that it was only by personally observing and dissecting each aspect of a critical

---

[1] *Gemba* is a Japanese term for "the actual place"; "going to the gemba" means to get a firsthand look, which in a manufacturing setting typically involves going to the shop floor. It is a common term and a key theme in the conversion of existing processes to Lean.

business process that he could truly eliminate wasteful or duplicative activities and optimize any given process in the service of a particular business goal.

Lately, Peter had been spending a good part of each day sending out his résumé and communicating within his professional network, but he still had plenty of time to glance around at the workings of his own household. Because he was between jobs, he and his wife, Mary, had shifted to cost-cutting mode in an effort to maintain their standard of living. Peter, therefore, had both the opportunity and the motivation to streamline and optimize the ways in which he and Mary purchased and used consumable goods. He considered this project not only necessary from a financial standpoint but also a way to exercise his professional skills. *No sense in allowing my game to slip*, he thought to himself.

One morning midweek, Peter was pulling several recycling containers out to the curb when he ran into his neighbor, Paul Wright, who was hauling his green bins out to the street at the same time. Paul was a consultant for a restructuring firm that helped streamline companies' operations while they were under bankruptcy protection. He didn't deal primarily with the financial underpinnings of a company; instead, he worked to improve operational efficiency where needed and appropriate for the bankruptcy workout plan. He was between assignments at the moment, as well, and preparing to head to Shanghai the following week to assist with a multinational company project there. Today, however, he was simply carting his recycling out to the curb like every other suburbanite.

Paul: How's it going? Got any leads yet?

Peter: A few, and I've got an interview next week with a large manufacturer, so that's promising. I'm really hoping to find something local. I don't know how you do it—always in a different city.

Paul: Yeah, it was great for the first 5 years, but the second 5 really dragged. I miss my family, and I've gotten so tired of living out of a suitcase! But this is my job, and I like what I do.

Peter: I hear you. It's a good thing, to like what you do. So ... that's a lot of newspapers.

Paul: It's my one wasteful habit, I must admit. I could be getting all my news online, but when I'm home, I like the homey feel of opening a newspaper and having a cup of coffee at my kitchen table with Beth. Why so many cans of cola?

Peter: Well, it's funny that you bring it up, because I've been wondering how to broach this topic with Mary. You know how plumbers' faucets are always leaky? And the shoemaker's kids need new shoes? Sometimes the hardest thing to do is apply what you know to yourself.

Paul: Yep, I'll agree with that.

Peter: So the issue is this: I'm not sure that Mary and I approach purchasing and inventory management at home properly. Otherwise, there wouldn't be almost 50 half-empty cans of cola in the recycling bins.

Paul: Well, why don't I just take a look, then! I can do a run-through on your house, and point out places where I think you could change your systems—and you can do the same with mine. We're both on the bench[2] this week, so why not?

---

[2] "On the bench" is a phrase used to describe a period of work inactivity, often for consultants between engagements.

Peter: Okay, sure! I'll make more coffee.
Paul: Perfect.

[*The men trudge up Peter's walkway and through the front door. The kitchen is relatively tidy. Peter busies himself setting up the coffeemaker and getting out the supplies—coffee grounds, a filter, water, cream, sugar, and cups. Paul, meanwhile, begins opening Peter's cabinets and perusing the contents of the refrigerator.*]

Peter: Find anything interesting?
Paul: Well, you're right about the cans of cola … Mary does buy a lot of it. How many does she drink a day?
Peter: I don't know, one or two, maybe. Why?
Paul: I was just thinking, you know, they sell those 8-ounce containers.
Peter: Don't get me wrong here—of course I want Mary to buy whatever she wants to drink. But from a monetary standpoint, wouldn't that be even more wasteful? I think those little cans cost more per ounce, right? She drinks only 6 ounces of cola regardless of which can she opens.
Paul: Well, even though the smaller can costs more per ounce, it costs less per can, so Mary's effective cost per ounce is lower for the smaller cans. Plus, she's throwing less away. Okay, then, let's keep opening your kitchen cabinets, and see if we can identify any more places in your purchasing patterns that look like they could use some improvement.

Peter: Aren't we forgetting something?

Paul: What?

Peter: Well, we need to define the term *improvement* for this context, right? Shouldn't we start by defining what my goals are in terms of my purchasing patterns, so we know what we're looking for as we go through the cabinets, and what something better might look like?

Paul: Good point. No use treating this as something casual. If we're spending time doing this, we may as well approach it the way we would a professional project. So what are your goals?

Peter: Well, I'd like to level out the purchasing spikes. Since Mary and I live within walking distance of a large retail grocery store, pharmacy, and plenty of restaurants, if we exhaust our supply of some commonly used item—like dishwashing detergent—then we can easily get more. Also, since the storage space in this house is in relatively short supply, my preference is to even out our supply of most items by buying only what we need.

Paul [shuffling through the cabinet under the sink]: Yes, wow, I see what you mean. Half of your space in this cabinet is occupied by gallons of cleaning supplies. Dishwasher detergent, liquid dish soap, hand soap, glass cleaner.... It would take you five years to go through all this!

Peter: You see what I mean? And buying the cleaners like that causes purchasing spikes, too. There's no sense in paying for five years' worth of detergent up front. It just doesn't make good business sense. By keeping that money in our bank account longer, it gives us an opportunity to invest it in something that will make money in the meantime.

Paul: Also, judging from the way stuff is packed in here so tightly, there's a problem with safety and usability. What happens in a production facility when the supply room is messy and unorganized? It's a safety hazard, for one thing, and it's not usable, for another. The operators can't find the maintenance supplies when they're needed, and as a result, the equipment doesn't get maintained the way it should. That ultimately affects everything in a business—from the rate of capital expenditure on replacement equipment to product quality to customer satisfaction.

Peter: I admit it, that cabinet needs to be cleaned out. It's ironic to me that it's full of cleaning supplies, since those go on sale all the time. So there's no point in storing three huge bottles of something when I can almost always find smaller quantities on sale at regular intervals. I just can't justify using up storage space with stock I don't really need.

Paul: That's true. For now, you could invest in some smaller, empty dispensing bottles, and store these large containers in your basement. Just fill up the smaller containers until the bulk ones are empty. Then you'd have a usable cabinet here. And, wow, do I see a fire extinguisher way back there? Just think, if there was a fire, you could actually reach that.

Peter: Not going to argue with you there.

Paul: I think I understand what your goals are, then: first, to level out the costs of your monthly purchases, and second, to limit bulk purchases to those items where it really makes sense, to generate some "working capital." What about the manner in which you and Mary go about making purchases? Are you happy with that process?

Peter: I think that could use some improvement too, Paul. I feel like Mary and I often come home with the same items, because each of us didn't realize that the other had time to swing by the store that day.

Paul: What you need is a visual management system.

Peter: I've thought about that too, but I don't want something so cumbersome that it wouldn't get used. Plus, this house is so small that I didn't want to waste any wall space.

Paul: What about a kanban system? It does look like you buy a lot of just a few items, so this might work well for you. These jars and cans are just stacked up in your pantry at random—probably because you were busy when you got home from the store and just needed to get them put away. You could arrange them a little more neatly, with the labels showing. That way it would be more obvious what you do and don't have in your cabinets.

Peter [inspired]: Or, we could stack the cans in rows, and as we use a can of tomato sauce just shift the cans in back to the front.

You know what that reminds me of? Once or twice, I've been with Mary at the local retail pharmacy when she wanted to buy a new lipstick or two. Have you seen those dispensers where you can fill up the stock of a particular shade of lipstick on the top, and then it dispenses out from the bottom? That is such an easy way to keep track of the stock of each lipstick color just by scanning the rows of dispensers to see what shades aren't there.

Paul: Ha! Yes, I think a kanban system might suit you just fine!

Peter [opening the other cabinet doors]: So, what's your verdict on the rest of it?

Paul: One thing I am noticing is that you own a lot of small kitchen appliances that are pushed back behind all these boxes of pasta and cans of tuna.

Peter: Yes, that was our wedding haul. Frankly, I wish we had time to use more of that stuff. But you know, half of them are missing pieces, or I can never find some part when I want to use the appliance, like the cap to the blender or the blades that go in the food processor. So it's almost as if they're not there.

Paul: Maybe you and Mary should go through them one weekend and sort out what the missing pieces are, and then develop a storage system so you know where to find everything. With all the storage space you'll be saving by buying for just a week's worth of food and supplies at a time, you can store a wider variety of foods and do a bit more cooking.

Peter: Great idea! I can just see her face when she walks in the door one rainy evening after a long day at work, and there's a candlelit table waiting, complete with flowers and a homemade meal! That's a perfect goal to work toward. I can see it now!

Paul: Excellent. Now all you have to do is hold that thought.

DETERMINING THE OPTIMAL LOT SIZE FOR HOUSEHOLD SUPPLIES

ECONOMIC ORDER QUANTITY (EOQ)

Lean Takeaways

A number of considerations are important to lot size, such as storage and shipping costs, usage patterns, and perishability. Quantity-discount savings may be spurious once total system costs are considered. Likewise, quantity ordered may be increased to save shipping costs. Inventory serves a strategic purpose as part of a Lean implementation: once we recognize its need, a visual management system is often optimal for monitoring the amount on hand.

In the next story, we will begin to think through optimizing inventory quantities by evaluating cost trade-offs.

The economic order quantity (EOQ) is a measurement that represents a judgment about the best amount of a process input, product, or component material that should be ordered at one time. It involves an assessment that balances the cost of holding inventory against the cost of obtaining it, which is sometimes described as the setup or ordering cost. This judgment should be made in alignment with an organization or entity's capabilities, operating systems design, and value proposition. Ideally, these three elements are already aligned because the leaders of the organization developed them with alignment in mind.

The concept of EOQ incorporates several cost components. The setup or ordering cost might include such obvious costs as ordering fees, flat-rate commissions, fixed shipping fees, or transportation costs—and it might also include other, intangible costs to acquisition, such as the cost to a relationship or the strain on a human network. The variable cost of holding inventory (i.e., the holding cost) is also considered when determining the EOQ. Other costs to excess inventory are shrinkage—in other words, the more inventory you have, the more possibility there is that someone will steal it; opportunity cost, meaning that the more money is tied up in inventory, the less cash is available for other projects, such as construction or capital expenses; and additional handling costs. Additional handling would be an example of the overprocessing that occurs when items need to be moved multiple times. Perhaps, because there is a large amount of inventory, an item must be accessed that is in the back of a large pile. It must be moved to the front or from store to store.

REORDER POINTS

Peter and Paul determine the amount of safety stock in soap and soda that they think the Orvilles will need. If they "order" too soon, they'll have too much—but if they order too late, they'll run out. They need to balance the cost of holding inventory against the cost of shortage. They discuss a reorder point decision when Peter mentions that he'll simply go to the store when he thinks he needs to.

In this context, the cost of shortage is manageable, since there is some tolerance for stock-out built into the system. The store is so close, and Peter's availability is so flexible, that the setup cost for obtaining new soap seems minimal. This all might change, however, when Peter finds a new job and isn't so focused on the contents of his cabinets!

The cost of holding inventory in this context is less related to security, insurance, and risk of theft (i.e., external factors that could lead to waste) than it is to physical limitations such as the capacity of their cabinets. Peter's goal is to have fresher, more varied foods, and cleaning supplies in smaller quantities. He thinks this will help him use his cabinets more efficiently, cook more meals at home, and have easy access to cleaning tools and safety-related items, such as fire extinguishers.

QUANTITY DISCOUNTS

What about Peter's conversation with Paul regarding his practices for ordering supplies for his home helps us understand the following:

- Economic order quantity (EOQ)?
- Quantity discount?
- Life cycle costing?
- Visual management systems?

Peter and his wife differ in their approach to purchasing. Mary prefers to buy items in bulk, sometimes with a quantity discount. The drawback to a bulk purchase is that the inventory must then be stored, maintained, and dispensed, and the cash required to make the initial purchase isn't then available for other projects—all of the typical considerations involved in an EOQ decision. Peter thinks that regularly priced items at the nonbulk retail grocery store are at least as good in terms of price and are sold in more convenient quantities. Spending less money up front also frees up those dollars to use on other things.

Peter has another EOQ conundrum related to quantity discounts. Peter's wife, Mary, drinks only 6 ounces from each can of cola that she opens. She purchases 12-ounce cans, which means she is wasting 6 ounces of each can she opens. The 12-ounce cans cost more per can than the 8-ounce cans, but the 8-ounce cans cost more per ounce. So if she were to drink 6 of the 8 ounces of a 8-ounce can, she'd be wasting fewer ounces of soda, even though those ounces cost more per ounce to purchase. If she begins purchasing the 8-ounce can, she will waste less soda and less money.

Quantity purchase decisions are driven by many of the same consideration as EOQ—and are a subset of EOQ decisions when a larger quantity purchase costs less per unit. Bulk purchase decisions are useful when the cost of holding inventory is minimal and the discount is high. For Peter, a large quantity of detergent would render his cleaning-fluid cabinet useless if the other types of cleaning products did not fit or were not accessible. Quantity discounts are simply one more factor included in the "setup" or "acquisition cost" side of the EOQ equation. The benefits of a quantity discount must still be balanced against all the same tangible and intangible factors, including:

- Shrinkage and spoilage (will it spoil or will anyone take it?)
- Carrying costs (what does it cost to store?)
- Opportunity cost (what if you can't afford the oil and fuel, because you've purchased so much detergent—or, worse, you can't invest in an important new project?)

EOQ decisions should relate to the value proposition of the organization. What are you in the business of doing—storing inventory or selling goods and services? If an organization's core competencies are in line with its value proposition, then decisions regarding inventory management and quantity purchases should flow more naturally from that understanding of an organization's mission and objectives.

VISUAL MANAGEMENT

One type of visual management system is a kanban. An example of a kanban system is provided in "David and the Case of the Hoarded House" in Chapter 9. David and Heidi use a kanban system as part of their 5S-inspired cleanout of their kitchen, closet, and garage. They rearrange their pantry supplies (canned goods, peanut butter, and jelly) so that the quantities are easily seen. As each jar or can is used, the others slide to the front. When only one jar is visible, then they know it's time to put the item on that week's grocery list. A kanban system can be an easy way to visually check inventory levels and, according to lead times and other factors, place orders so that the item will be in stock as often as possible.

Peter also considers using a kanban system in his kitchen. Paul notices that he tends to buy larger quantities of just a few items. Because of this, it might be easy for Peter to arrange the jars or cans in rows, sliding the back items toward the front as the new ones are used. This would likely make it easier for Peter and Mary to know when to put an item on the grocery list for that week—and help prevent overstock or stock-out in the process. Finally, the friends discuss a few different types of kanban systems, including the holders often used to dispense lipstick shades from the bottom that are refilled from the top. Not only do these systems make it easier to keep track of many different items that all generally look the same, but they also facilitate reordering.

BRAIN PLAY

1. What should Peter and Mary do to continue to improve their system for managing household supplies?
2. How could a church, synagogue, or mosque use the principles of lot size and supply-chain-management thinking to coordinate needed supplies?
3. Think about a situation in your personal or professional life wherein a shared visual management system would be helpful. How would you design and implement the system? Who would you include? What would you measure?

CHAPTER 15

Order Quantities and Safety Stock

BRAD AND GINA AND BABY MAKE THREE

Brad and Gina McClain were expecting their first baby and were trying to adjust to the many lifestyle changes that would soon be required of them. Their tiny third-floor walkup on the Lower East Side of Manhattan had already been challenging to navigate for Gina, who was in her seventh month, but she had persevered, assuring Brad that the extra exercise kept her fit and provided an opportunity for her to practice her advance-planning techniques. Who wanted to trudge back up six flights of stairs for a forgotten wallet?

Gina McClain, Tina Thomas, and Lena Robinson are sharing stories at Gina's baby shower. Gina thinks through the decisions she and her husband must make in order to optimize the availability of diapers and other baby-care items in their apartment.

As you read Gina's story, think about the trade-offs involved in determining how many supplies she will keep on hand at once, and how her decisions might be different from those of her friends. In what ways could two people make different decisions in the same situation, given the same information?

Gina's best friends, Tina Thomas and Lena Robinson, were having a baby shower for her on the Upper West Side. It was a happy day, but Gina's impending logistical reality loomed large in her mind and detracted from her enjoyment. She began to open the gifts, which were piled high on a table, and decided to broach with her friends one of her concerns: diapers.

Gina: It's not about the diaper changing. My main concern is how I will ever fit an adequate stash of diapers in our apartment. How do you know how many diapers to get at a time? We have less than 450 square feet in two rooms. The bathroom is tiny. I keep my shoes on shelves tucked up next to the ceiling! Where can I put everything and still have access to it?

Tina: I don't know how you do it. You've been to our house. It's Connecticut—space is not an issue. I just get in the SUV every couple of weeks and bring home everything I need from the warehouse club.

MT '12

Lena: Do you pass a convenience store on the way home from work?

Gina: Brad does.

Lena: Next time he passes by, just ask him to check the prices on diapers—he may be able to purchase a small amount every day or two.

Gina: That could work. And if I'm lucky, it might occur to him to pick up more than one thing while he's there.

Lena: So it seems to me that you have to figure out how to conveniently make frequent trips to the store and remember to only pick up one package at a time. As far as running out, can you afford not to store a package somewhere, in case of emergency? Maybe you don't ever let your diaper stash dip below, say, one day's worth of diapers—what is that, eight or nine?—in case Brad works late and can't make it on the planned day. Then one of you can go to the store the next day.

MT '12

Gina: That sounds like a plan. Good thinking!

Tina: That system really could apply to anything you need to keep in stock for baby care, like jars of baby food or children's pain reliever. I always keep a spare bottle up high on a shelf, because you never know when a cold or the flu will strike, and you'll reach into the everyday first-aid box and your bottle will be empty.

Lena: Or worse, sticky—all over the rest of your first-aid supplies, and the box!

Tina: That too. Except I ran into a problem once. My whole family caught the flu last year. I thought I was the queen bee mother, bringing down my secret cache of children's pain reliever from the top shelf. Wouldn't you know, the medicine had expired a year before! I had to ask Jeff to go out and get some in the middle of the night.

Gina: How often do you stop at a gas station? When your tank's half full? When it's on empty? When you see a lower price than you expected, just to top off your tank? What's the most cost-effective way to do that?

Lena: Take the subway! [*They laugh.*]

Gina: Actually, I have a motorcycle! I keep it parked in a friend's driveway in New Jersey. If I need to use it, it would be a similar situation to what we've planned for the diapers. I only buy what I need for that day's trip. I don't even fill the tank, because I never know how long it will be before I'll use it again. Being pregnant sure has put a damper on my road-warrior activities.

Lena: What about you, Tina?

Tina: Well, I'm as close to a hoarder as you can get without qualifying for the TV show. I'll go shop when I see a deal, and I keep my tank as full as possible at all times. In fact, when I bought my SUV, I opted for the extra gas tank. It can hold 32 gallons.

Lena: Good for you. You're ready for the apocalypse.

Tina: What about you, Lena? What's your purchase personality?

Lena: Well, Keith tends to make larger purchases—he'll catch a deal on plums or long-sleeved shirts or whatever—and all that starts to pile up, but he's good about buying stuff we actually use. I mostly buy on impulse. So sue me. But I've learned to control that by restricting the *amount* of whatever it is I'm buying.

Tina: What does that mean?

Lena: I don't buy large amounts. I stop at the market on the way home and just get what looks fresh and make that for dinner. We rarely have leftovers, and I don't keep much in the fridge at all. It's New York. I can get anything I want 24 hours a day. Plus, with both of us traveling for work all the time, it doesn't make sense to keep much in the apartment except our favorite things. Of course, when he finds a deal, he buys a lot of it!

Gina: Food for thought, certainly. Speaking of which, I'm eating for two. Do they sell falafels on Columbus Avenue?

THE IMPACT OF COST ESTIMATES ON PURCHASING DECISIONS

ECONOMIC ORDER QUANTITY (EOQ)

Lean Takeaways

A Lean culture prioritizes the minimization of inventory, but not at the expense of meeting customer requirements. The relative costs of stocking out of and holding inventory must be considered.

This ends the section on coordination, which encompasses the considerations involved in interacting with suppliers. Next, we discuss the primary elements of context and culture—the success of any operation depends upon the people.

The EOQ is the best (typically, most economical) amount of something that should be ordered at one time. As we learned in "Peter Goes Shopping" in Chapter 14, EOQ is a measurement that represents a judgment—a determination as to the optimal amount of a process input, product, or component material that should be ordered at one time. It involves an assessment that balances the cost of holding inventory against the cost of obtaining it, which is sometimes described as the setup cost. This judgment should be made in alignment with an organization or entity's capabilities, operating systems design, and value proposition. Ideally, these three elements are aligned when the leaders of the organization develop them.

The costs and potential benefits of setting an order quantity may include sources of nonfinancial value. Time, energy, attention, relationship capital, opportunity cost, and the waste associated with either excess inventory or the excess motion required to obtain inventory are examples of noneconomic factors that can influence EOQ. Another important step is collaborating with stakeholders to produce additional value for both buyer and seller.

SETUP COST

The *setup cost* is the total "hassle" of getting a process ready or acquiring something new. The time, money, attention, and other resources required to transport goods, change over a machine, get to the store, conduct a transaction, or have a sales conversation with a salesperson are all examples of setup cost. Lena recommends that Gina's husband, Brad, purchase diapers at a store he passes by on foot each day on the way home from work. This is a technique for avoiding or minimizing setup cost—incorporate the setup cost for one activity (transport to and from work) with another activity (purchases). It also minimizes the setup costs of "diaper acquisition" for Brad and Gina. Frequent purchases begin to make sense as part of the equation balancing setup cost, holding cost, opportunity cost, and total product cost. For Tina, however, the setup cost of driving to, navigating, and checking out of a warehouse store is a substantial investment—as a result, she makes less frequent trips and makes purchases in greater amounts.

HOLDING COST

Balancing the cost of acquiring something and the cost of stocking out of it against the cost of holding it is the key to EOQ. Gina says, "Gasoline … could go bad if you let it sit in storage containers, and it's inconvenient to store, so it's not something people usually purchase in advance." The inconvenience (cost, storage space capacity, security, climate control, etc.), spoilage cost (gas could "go bad"), as well as opportunity cost (what else could you be doing with that same amount of money or same amount of storage space?) together comprise the holding cost of any particular item. The holding cost of purchasing "too many" diapers, for Brad and Gina, primarily took the form of opportunity cost—the opportunity represented by the extremely limited storage space in their third-floor walkup. Storing large amounts of diapers wasn't a good solution for Brad and Gina because they needed the space.

SAFETY STOCK

The key question to answer when setting a level of safety stock is "What is the cost of not having what you want, when you want it?" Safety stock levels are influenced by setup cost, holding cost, opportunity cost, risk tolerance, and other factors. It should be based upon the above factors *as well as* a prediction of two less determinate but very important numbers: customer service level and forecasted demand variability.

How could Gina, Tina, and Lena's conversation at the baby shower about trade-offs help us determine the following:

- Economic order quantity?
- Reorder point?

The customer service level is expressed as a percentage. It answers the question "What percentage of the time that a customer wants to buy an item would you like to have it in stock?" The customer service level—97 percent, for example—means that 97 percent of the time, you plan to have the item in stock when a customer wants to buy it. And 3 percent of the time, the customer will be turned away empty-handed and you may lose sales or even repeat business. This is a decision that is important from an order-winning criteria (OWC) perspective.

Forecasted demand variability is a measure of how much demand is expected to fluctuate in the future. While no one can know the future, we often base our estimates of future variability on our records of past variability. Demand for diapers on any given day cannot be determined precisely—after all, this varies due to the general human condition. You can look at historic demand variability and, based on that, make a determination of what you *think* the demand will be in the future. If there were no variability in demand and the baby always needed 10 diapers per day, no more and no less, then no safety stock would be needed at all! Brad could simply purchase 10 new ones on his way home each day. But if there is any variability in either demand or lead time (for instance, perhaps the store is closed on Mondays), then safety stock is required as insurance against stock-out—but only to the degree that you wish to avoid incurring the costs of stock-out (i.e., customer service level).

Cycle stock is the stock that is used up due to normal demand between deliveries. If Gina estimates her daily diaper use at around 10 per day, and Brad plans to visit the convenience store to purchase diapers on a daily basis, then the cycle time is one day and the typical number of diapers used during the cycle time is also 10. If Brad were planning to visit the convenience store only every other day, then the typical number of diapers used during the cycle time would be 2 days × 10 diapers, or 20 diapers of *cycle stock*. If diapers were ordered only once a month, the number of diapers used (on average) would be 30 days × 10 diapers = 300 diapers of *cycle stock*. The cycle stock is the amount purchased and expected to be used between deliveries.

Brad and Gina discuss a reorder point decision when Gina mentions that she will calculate an average number of diapers needed per day, and they make sure to keep at least that much on hand—in case Brad cannot get to the store one day. She'll keep an alternative product, cloth diapers, on hand for emergencies. In doing so, she reduces the potential risk of shortage.

Reorder points (ROP) in the business world depend on context as well. An ROP decision should reflect organizational goals and support the value proposition. Safety stock is typically set at a higher point when the risk tolerance is lower and stock-out is to be avoided due to a higher customer service level. Some of the same less tangible costs that are part of the EOQ are also embedded in the ROP, such as the following:

- **Opportunity cost**: A higher level of safety stock or a higher reorder point also means more inventory, which is less liquid than cash.
- **Cost of overprocessing**: More safety stock can be more cumbersome or more difficult to organize. The risk of moving or handling an item more than once increases, as well as the costs to doing so.
- **Cost of spoilage and shrinkage**: The more inventory, the more there is of it that might disappear or become damaged.

INVENTORY MANAGEMENT POLICIES

The last three stories allowed us to look at inventory management policies from a number of different perspectives. Trade-offs that our protagonists considered included the cost of holding versus the cost of a stock-out, and the cost of ordering versus the cost of holding inventory. We also saw two different types of management systems—a reorder point (ROP) system and a periodic review (PR) system. We used two visuals for these two systems: the wave, and the coffee-serving waitress who always wants your cup to be full. Regardless of the system used, the actual decisions that are made with respect to order quantities and safety stock will depend on the individual's or the organization's estimates of the cost parameters and their tolerance toward risk. Many solutions are possible, and the selection depends on the perceived importance of various outcomes. This is the leadership point of view.

BRAIN PLAY

1. What else can Gina and Brad do to accomplish their goal of optimizing their purchase decisions?
2. How could a large electronics retailer use this thinking to establish procedures for ordering and maintaining inventory from multiple suppliers?
3. Think about a situation in your personal or professional life where the use of these Lean tools would be appropriate. Briefly describe the implementation steps.

PART V

Context and Culture

CHAPTER 16

Enabling Rational Decision Making

ZEKE'S TREE

Zeke Harrison walked home from the bus and negotiated his backpack through the front door. His father, Norman, a business school professor, put aside some papers he was grading and made sure the fifth grader did the three things he always did when he got home: take his shoes off and leave them by the door, empty out his lunchbox at the sink, and lay his school books on his desk. Norman encouraged Zeke to complete his homework right away; it made the remainder of the day easier for everyone, and Zeke had an easier time finishing everything up when it was still fresh in his mind.

Zeke Harrison, a fifth grader, has forgotten his vocabulary list and invents a way to complete his homework anyway. His father, Norman, helps him consider several possible courses of action and analyze them according to outcome and probability. Zeke is able to make a determination regarding his best course of action.

As you read, think about the process Norman used to enable Zeke to reach his own conclusions. Would you have evaluated the relative risks in the same way that Zeke did? What process did Norman use to empower Zeke to resolve his own problem?

Norman: Hi Zeke! How was your day?
Zeke: Fine.
Norman: What's your homework?
Zeke: Well, I finished the math in class. Our teacher gave us a few minutes, and it was simple today. Pre-algebra is so totally easy.

Norman [looking askance at his son]: Well, I'm glad you think so. I'm going to check over what you did anyway, just to make sure. What else?

Zeke: The only other thing is this vocabulary thing [*looking for the assignment in the notebook*]. There's this story we're reading, "Ten Ways to Slice Bread," and I was supposed to write down 10 words that are new to me and look up the definitions. I already have the list of words. There's a quiz on them tomorrow. The book report is for next week.

Norman: That's it? That's the only assignment? Man, you got off lucky today. Is there anything you can do in advance tonight, so you can spread out your homework load over the week?

Zeke [still looking around for the assignment]: You mean, like start an outline for the book report?

Norman: Great idea. I'm proud of you. I'm so proud, in fact, that I'm going to make you some popcorn to eat while you work.

Zeke [looks up]: I guess I'm starting the book report.

Norman: I'll be back to check on you in a minute. [*Norman gets up and heads into the kitchen.*]

Zeke [groans loudly]: AAAAAUUUGH!

Norman [from kitchen]: What?

Zeke: The list of words isn't in here. I left it at school or on the bus or something.

Norman: Can't you just call somebody?

Zeke [exasperated]: Dad—I told you! Each kid had to come up with their own words! Nobody has the same list! I can't find my list!

Norman: Okay, okay, take it easy. We can solve the problem together if we think it through.

Zeke [visibly frustrated]: Well, they were right here a minute ago! I don't get it! I know I put them in this folder!

Norman: Can we e-mail Ms. Senn?

Zeke: She might not check her e-mail! I'm stuck! I'll get a zero!

Norman [coming back from kitchen]: Well, what are your options?

Zeke: Nothing! There are no options! I can't do anything!

Norman [sitting back down next to his son]: Zeke, I can help you figure this out. And you know the place you always start is by thinking about your options.

Zeke [slumping down in his chair]: Like not do anything?

Norman: And what would the result of that choice be?

Zeke: Bad.

Norman: Is that all?

Zeke: Ms. Senn would not be happy. She would be disappointed. So that would be horrible.

Norman [pulls a piece of loose-leaf paper out of Zeke's notebook and begins drawing a diagram, Exhibit 1]: I think it would make it easier if you looked at it on a piece of paper. We'll draw this box. The box means you have a decision to make. The lines coming out of the box will be options. Here's the "Do Nothing" option, here at the top, and next to it is the result you'd get if you chose that option, "Horrible." Agreed?

Zeke [grateful his father is not drawing on a napkin]: Agreed.

Norman: So what's the next choice?

Zeke: I guess I could try to remember the words.

Norman: Great. We'll put that choice here. Now what are the possible outcomes of that choice? There are probably more than one.

Zeke [beginning to calm down]: Well, I could remember just a few of them, or only some of them, or all of them.

Norman: And the results for each of those, I suppose, would be "Horrible," "Fair," and "Great," in that order. [*Zeke nods again.*] Now we have to assign percentages to each of these probabilities. If this is a complete set of possible outcomes, then one of these must occur. What do the probabilities have to add up to?

Zeke [looking at his dad like he's a fool]: 100 percent, duh.

Norman: Okay. What do you think your chances are of guessing all the words correctly?

Zeke: I don't know, maybe 50 percent?

Norman: You got it. Good. Okay, so what are the chances that you'll guess only some of the words correctly?

Zeke: Well, it can just be the other 50 percent, because I know I'll remember at least some of them. We just had this class today.

Norman [scribbling]: Okay, sure. So the third option, remembering none of the words, is a zero. That means if you try to remember them yourself, you have a 50 percent chance of each of these outcomes. We'll draw that on the chart with each of the outcomes coming out of a dot. What's the next option?

Zeke: I could try to e-mail Ms. Senn and just work on that outline for the book report. Then we could wait for Ms. Senn to e-mail me back. But she might not check her e-mail.

Norman: Good thinking. So the possible outcomes of that choice might be "Horrible" if she doesn't e-mail us back or "Pretty Good" if she does, because then you'd have all the words, not just some of them.

Zeke: Yeah, but she probably won't check her e-mail, so out of 100 percent, I'd say there's a 95 percent chance that she won't write us back tonight.

Norman: Okay, so that leaves a 5 percent chance that she will. And the results of those outcomes would be 95 percent "Horrible" and 5 percent "Pretty Good."

Zeke [face lighting up]: There is another option...

Norman: What's that?

Zeke: Well, I have the book right here where I found the words. What if I just made up a new list of words that I don't know?

Norman [sitting back in his chair]: Well, that is a possibility, you're right. And I bet there's an additional benefit to that choice, because it will help you think about the outline you want to write for that book report.

Zeke: So the possible outcomes of that will be either Ms. Senn will be happy that I looked up words I didn't know and solved my own problem, or she won't like it that I changed the words.

Norman: True, that's true. So what are the probabilities?

Zeke: A 70 percent chance that she's happy, which is a "Pretty Good" and 30 percent chance that she's mad, which is "Horrible."

Norman: That sounds about right—much more likely that she'd be happy that you took the initiative to make a new list. So what are you going to choose?

Zeke: Well, that one, Dad.

Norman [getting up]: Great choice. That calls for popcorn.

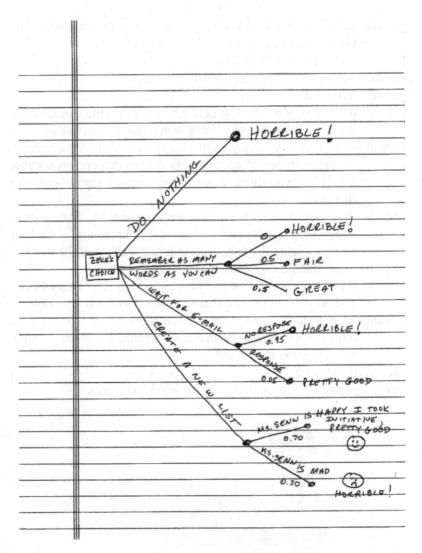

DATA SOURCE: ZEKE'S FATHER

DECISION ANALYSIS FOR HOMEWORK SUCCESS: EMPOWERING HOMEWORK COMPLETION USING DECISION TREES

DECISION ANALYSIS

Every organization or individual has a process by which risk is assessed and acted upon. This process should ideally be intentional and strategic in nature. Leaders make strategic choices regarding risk management process when they learn about what "success" or "failure" means to their customers. It is the potential success or failure of any decision—from the point of view of the customer—that should be evaluated when making decisions.

Leaders can listen to the voice of the customer (VOC) by designing methods for conversation, such as through social media and focus groups. This helps build trust with customers and respond more quickly to changes in customer needs and viewpoints.

Lean Takeaways

Lean is about more than the tools in a Lean toolbox and how and when they can be best applied. The most successful Lean conversions involve developing people through a collaborative problem-solving process. Educating Lean participants in a systematic method for evaluating several different approaches to solving a problem helps build participant confidence and supports a culture of using metrics as a means of making decisions.

The quality of Zeke's solution and its likelihood of success were improved due to his involvement in the generation and evaluation of decision alternatives. Steps for evaluating a decision can be created to help walk someone through a decision process. When used in this way, "standard work" can be used to structure problem solving.

In Chapter 17, we will further investigate methods for gaining employee engagement in the context of day-to-day operations.

Zeke's customer is his teacher, and while "learning" might be his father's priority, "pleasing the teacher" is Zeke's number one goal. Each of the outcomes he considers to be important is related to whether or not his teacher will be satisfied with his decision-making process and work product. Zeke thinks about the VOC when he builds a process for evaluating the risks of his decision.

Businesses operationalize decision-making processes when they define a hurdle rate for new projects, for instance, or when they link new product development, resource allocation, or cost-cutting decisions to the preferences of their customers.

DECISION TREES

Decision trees are visual representations of the VOC. They are a systematic way of assessing the risk and probability of various outcomes—those outcomes being the effect of various decisions on one's customers. Each form of risk can be considered, including whether or not some of the risk can be reduced. Zeke's decision tree is based on the response of his teacher to his various options: "Try to remember the words" or "Make up a new list." The outcomes "Horrible" and "Pretty Good" all refer to his teacher's possible reaction when she sees what he has done.

Why does Norman and Zeke's conversation about homework angst help us understand the following:

- Decision analysis?
- Decision trees?
- Creating operational capabilities and value?
- The Socratic method
- Risk mitigation?

Let's take a superficially unrelated business problem: should we purchase Machine A, which will increase our capacity by 15 percent but decrease our overall quality by 5 percent? Or should we purchase Machine B, which will decrease our capacity by 5 percent but raise our overall quality by 15 percent? The best decision tree would be built around customer behavior and preferences. What does the customer care about? Quantity or quality?

THE SOCRATIC METHOD

Norman realizes that the ultimate goal is not getting Zeke's homework done, but rather that Zeke develop the ability to solve problems on his own. Similarly, the goal of education should not be the rote memorization of facts, but rather the ability to handle unanticipated and ambiguous situations. The process that Norman uses provides Zeke with a new tool and allows him to solve the current problem on his own. This provides two benefits: (1) Zeke will be more likely to accept the current solution, and (2) he will likely be able to address future problems on his own.

The futurist Alvin Toffler is quoted as saying, "Tomorrow's illiterate will not be the man who can't read; he will be the man who has not learned how to learn." Another great thinker, Eric Hoffer, said, "In a world of change, the learners shall inherit the earth, while the learned shall find themselves perfectly suited for a world that no longer exists."

Similar to Norman's goal for Zeke, organizations must create a culture where employees are constantly growing and can solve problems on their own. Norman has done this by repeatedly asking questions, and allowing Zeke to determine not only his options but also the possible outcomes and probabilities. This approach is similar in some ways to the Toyota philosophy, in that they "manufacture people and not cars"—people who are trained in the Toyota Production System and its problem-solving techniques.

THE CHANGE EFFECTIVENESS EQUATION

This book contains no equations except Little's Law and this one, the Change Effectiveness Equation, which is not really an equation because it can't be solved with numbers. It is, rather, a relationship that exists between the *q*uality of a solution, the *a*cceptance of that solution by the people involved in implementing it, and the *e*ffectiveness of the change effort. The equation looks like this:

$$E = Q \times A$$

What is important to remember is that the solution might be the most perfect solution ever; if the people involved in implementing the solution don't accept it, then the results won't be effective. Conversely, the people involved in implementing a solution might be ready to go and completely accepting of the change; yet if the solution isn't very good, then the results also won't be effective. You need both: the solution has to be of a high quality, and the people implementing it need to accept the solution and the need to change. These are the conditions that yield the best results.

This "equation" has been written about by General Electric. A team explored the reasons why big-change projects can fail, paying particular attention to technology upgrades and other projects that were intended to improve internal processes. They discovered that insufficient cultural acceptance of the change was generally the most important reason for failure, rather than the quality of the solution.[1]

---

[1] http://bvonderlinn.wordpress.com/2009/01/25/overview-of-ges-change-acceleration-process-cap/

This equation also uses multiplication and not addition. In other words, if *a*cceptance is zero, then the results will always be zero as well—because zero multiplied by anything is also a zero. If this were an equation using addition, then the *e*ffectiveness of the solution would be the *sum* of the *q*uality and the acceptance—but this is not how the equation is written. Instead, if either the quality or the acceptance is zero, then the effectiveness of the solution will also be zero.

In this story, any solution that Zeke and Norman create will be more effective the higher Zeke's acceptance of the solution. Involving him in the decision-making process increases the likeliness of his acceptance of the solution and therefore increases the probability of a successful outcome.

BRAIN PLAY

1. How can Norman decide which decisions are appropriate for Zeke to make and which are not?
2. In which industries is employee engagement a competitive advantage?
3. Think about a situation in your personal or professional life wherein enabling someone else to make decisions that affect you would be appropriate. What training would you need? How would you evaluate results?

CHAPTER 17

Analyzing Root Causes

JACKSON AND WYATT LEARN TO SHARE

Rebecca Tilden, a 2003 MBA graduate, had two boys: Jackson, who was 8 years old, and Wyatt, who was 6 years old. The two brothers were kids with tons of enthusiasm. They worked hard in school and played equally hard at home. After returning from after-school care in the evenings, they practiced various martial arts skills together for hours.

Rebecca Tilden is needlessly interrupted when her two sons, Jackson (age 8) and Wyatt (age 6), squabble over a hammock. The boys' inability to independently take turns is both an impediment to their social development and what Rebecca considers to be a "defect" in her family's normal operations.

As you read Rebecca's story, think about what she did to build consensus.

Often, the boys both wanted to do the same thing at the same time, whether it was resting in the hammock, playing with a basketball, or drawing with a particular green marker. After a few shouts of "Mine!" and "No, I want it!" one boy would escalate the altercation by practicing a martial arts skill a little *too* hard. As a result, Rebecca frequently found herself settling disputes that she felt they ought to resolve independently.

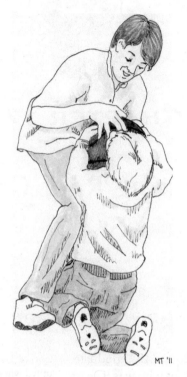

In graduate school, Rebecca had conducted a number of field studies in the area of continuous process improvement, and she considered communication an essential ingredient in the success of any process improvement program. She often used this experience in coping with situations at home because she thought the dynamics of her family and the dynamics of a corporation were much the same.

For instance, one evening after work, Rebecca was taking a shower when Wyatt banged on the door of the bathroom. She could hear him crying as he called her.

Wyatt: Mommy! Mommy! Jackson punched me!

Rebecca: Wyatt, I'm getting out of the shower. This is my alone time. Can you work out this problem by yourself?

Wyatt: No! You have to come give him a time-out! He stole the hammock from me! It's my turn!

Rebecca: Wyatt, go back outside and talk to your brother. I'll be there in a minute. I have lots of jobs that are important to being your mommy, but judging every argument is not one of them. I expect you and Jackson to share. Now, go outside, and I will be there soon.

Wyatt: Okay.

Wyatt trotted outside and waited. Rebecca dressed and walked down the steps to the backyard. She likened this moment to "pulling the andon cord" in a Toyota factory. She realized that the communication between the boys was defective and needed to be improved.

Rebecca: Okay, guys. Let's have a family meeting.

Boys: Okay.

Rebecca: Boys, you will be brothers forever. You will be living together for the next 12 years. Sometimes there will be two or three of something, and you will not have to share. But I can guarantee you that there will **always** be times when there is only *one* of something.

Jackson: Like right now. It's my turn to sit in the hammock.

Rebecca: Yes, that's true. Like right now.

Wyatt: But Mommy, it's my turn.

Rebecca: Will you help me figure out a way to solve this problem by thinking about it together? [*Both boys nod.*]

Rebecca: Do either of you know of a problem-solving skill that you can use when there's only one of something?

Jackson: You can take turns.

Wyatt: My turn is first.

Rebecca: Taking turns is a good idea. But how will you decide whose turn is first? What's a good way to decide that?

Wyatt: You can flip a coin. I'm heads.

Jackson: NO! I'M HEADS!

Rebecca: Let's decide who is heads and who is tails right now.

Jackson: He can be heads. I'll be tails.

Rebecca: Thank you, Jackson. That was very nice of you. You helped the family find a solution by being willing to give something up.

Jackson: But I'm first on the hammock.

Rebecca [ignoring this interjection]: Okay, guys. Let's review. We decided that a good way to share was to take turns, and a good way to decide whose turn is first is to flip a coin. Great start. Now, let's decide how long a turn will be.

Wyatt: Maybe 10 minutes?

Jackson: No, 15 minutes, and I go first!

Rebecca: Everybody's turn has to be the same amount of time, so it's fair. If Jackson's turn is 15 minutes, so is Wyatt's turn. The longer the turns, the longer you have to wait. What do you guys say to 10 minutes as a trial? We can always change it if that's too short.

Wyatt: Okay, 10 minutes.

Jackson: Oh, all right, Mom. But you take his side on *everything*.

Rebecca: I'm sorry it seems like that, honey. It's not true, but it might feel like that sometimes.

Wyatt: Let's flip a coin. Where's the coin?

Rebecca: Why don't we hide quarters all over the house and yard in special places? That way you always have a coin when you need one, and you don't have to go looking around in my purse. You can do it yourselves. What do you think about that?

Jackson: Can I put them around the yard?

Rebecca: Sure you can. Now, let's finish this by taking a family vote. If you vote "yes," you're committing to using this process *every* time you need to share something for the next month. It's May 15, so that means that I will put June 15 on the calendar as our "review" date. In exactly one month, we can evaluate our new process and decide if it worked or if we need to change parts of it to make it work. So if you vote "yes" now, you're only committing to one month, not forever. You can change your mind later if this trial doesn't feel right to you. How does that sound to you guys?

Wyatt: Mommy, I don't understand.

Rebecca: Raise your hand if you vote to flip a coin to decide who gets the first 10-minute turn *every* time you need to share something until June 15th. [*Hands fly up in the air and collide.*]

Rebecca: Yay! We solved our problem! Great family meeting, guys! In one month, we can decide if this was a good solution or not, okay?

Boys: Okay, Mommy!

Jackson: I'm first on the hammock.

Wyatt: Flip the coin, Mommy.

Rebecca: You flip it, Wyatt.

Wyatt [flips coin; it's tails]: I guess you're first, Jackson. But I'm next!

BUILDING FAMILY CONSENSUS
THROUGH ROOT CAUSE ANALYSIS

ANDON CORDS

In the Toyota Production System, the andon cord is an actual cord that any worker not only can but *should* pull if there is a problem that could impact product quality or workstation safety. Pulling the cord means that production is stopped temporarily while all the workers help to solve the problem before the production line is restarted. This practice is thought to eliminate defects on the line. In this story, the defect occurs during the process of playtime. Rebecca is disturbed unnecessarily when her children, Jackson and Wyatt, cannot decide for themselves how to share.

Problems within the "processes" of a relationship can occur in everyday life, just as mechanical or delivery process problems can occur on an assembly line. Regardless of the context, process disruptions can negatively impact outcomes. When Jackson and Wyatt create a process to help them share, it is important to consider each boy's interpersonal style and consider whether these styles work well together.

Some people use the equivalent of a

Lean Takeaways

Lean requires employee involvement and empowerment in order to achieve process improvement. Collective problem solving can often result in conflicting views about the best ways to approach or resolve an identified issue. In this story, Rebecca works with her sons to develop a standard process for conflict resolution, which can be helpful as a cultural part of an organization's Lean processes and infrastructure.

Another insight presented by this story is the concept of the andon cord—a real or metaphorical cord that can be pulled to stop production. In the Toyota Production System, employees pull the andon cord to stop the manufacturing lines and gather around the source of a defect to try to resolve it in real time. In this story, Rebecca identified an interpersonal struggle as a "defect" in communication and family functioning, and she pulled the andon cord so that the family could fix the problem and move on.

The first 17 stories addressed specific Lean tools. Yet the essence of any Lean conversion is the process of change management itself. In the next and final story (Chapter 18), we discuss some frameworks for leading strategic change. A true Lean conversion must be strategic with respect to changing the culture and maximizing the value-creating potential of the organization.

threshold or upper-specification limit for deciding how to manage disagreements. For example, disagreements might be dealt with as they arise, or they might be overlooked until they reach a certain level. Some people might have an absolute no-tolerance policy for certain types of behavior, while other behaviors might be allowed to persist unless they conflict with something else that's more important. Sometimes, one person solves problems one way—perhaps prioritizing keeping the peace, and waiting until a certain degree of "problem" is reached before reaching for the andon cord and halting the action—while another prioritizes resolving problems as they come up and then moving on.

ROOT CAUSE ANALYSIS

Root cause analysis attempts to address actual causes of problems rather than symptoms. People often jump to conclusions about root causes and end up frustrated when their countermeasures do not solve the actual problems. One series of steps that can be used to identify root causes is as follows:

1. Identify the high-level or immediate problem.
2. What are the many possible causes?
3. What are the most likely causes?
4. Where are the most likely origins of those causes?
5. Ask the five whys (discussed below).
6. Identify the possible root cause(s).

The boys ask "Why?" several times to discover the "real" reason behind their need to disturb their mother. Root cause analysis typically involves a systematic uncovering of the "real root" of a problem. The problem is viewed as a symptom or surface manifestation of an underlying problem that is less obvious. Asking "Why?" five times in a sequence is one traditional means of identifying the most useful way of looking at a problem.

One classic example of this is the failure of a machine on a production line. A shop floor employee might pull the andon cord in response to noticing a problem in production. For instance, the circle that the machine was supposed to stamp in a flat sheet of aluminum might be off-center beyond a certain acceptable distance. When the andon cord is pulled, the production line stops, and the employees gather to discuss the underlying reasons that might have been the cause of this off-center circle. They then ask "Why?" five times in a row. The dialogue might sound something like this:

Q1: Why did the machine stamp a circle that is off-center?
A: Because the calibration was off.

Q2: Why was the calibration off?
A: It was set correctly yesterday. It must have drifted from its initial set position.

Q3: Why could it have drifted?
A: Because there was too much oil.

Q4: Why was there too much oil?
A: Because the oil distributor is not working properly.

Q5: Why does the oil distributor not work properly?
A: Because it was not maintained properly.

In a perfect world, the oil distributor is replaced, the machine is restored to a state in which it can produce circles within a given acceptable range, and the production line resumes its busy uptime state. In reality, sometimes the root cause is identified within two or three questions, and sometimes the root cause can never be identified. Another possibility is that once the root cause is identified, it is not cost-effective to address it—and symptomatic causes are addressed instead. The leadership component of these decisions lies in understanding what different root causes exist and making informed decisions about where, when, and how to invest resources in correcting them.

Rebecca, Jackson, and Wyatt conduct their root cause, or five whys analysis, like this:

Q1: Why did you boys feel like you had to come and get me?
A: Because we were in a fight.

Q2: Why were you in a fight?
A: Because he wouldn't give me a turn. [*Wyatt points to his older brother.*]

Q3: Jackson, did you let him take his turn? If not, why not?
A: It wasn't that I wouldn't let him take his turn, Mommy. He wouldn't let me take my turn. It was my turn.

Q4: Why couldn't you boys take turns?
A: Because we didn't share.

Q5: Why didn't you share with each other?
A: We don't know how to decide who goes first.

What insights can we gain from Rebecca's conversation with her children about learning to share that can help us understand the following:

- Andon cords?
- Root cause analysis?
- Employee teamwork?

This root cause analysis has less to do with a mechanized process than it does with the relationship processes that exist between all of us—even, and perhaps especially, coworkers. Intangible sources of process delay or disruption might be at play that essentially are miscommunications between people. This is not surprising, since the human factor in almost any organization is at once its source of energy, strength, vitality, and direction *and* its frequent source of conflict.

When two or more individuals are necessary to complete a process but they disagree, it is difficult to know where to draw the line between "smoothing things over" and "getting to the root of a problem." Personality conflicts are often best left to the individuals to sort out between themselves—whereas conflicts affecting the organization's ability to deliver on its value proposition can be sorted out in the same manner that any root cause is revealed and corrected. When the focus of any root cause discussion is kept on the work product and the process at hand, then the improvement efforts can remain targeted on the desired outcome.

EMPLOYEE TEAMWORK AS PART OF CONTINUOUS PROCESS IMPROVEMENT

Rebecca and the boys work together to resolve the problem of unnecessary disruption of play. The practices of pulling the andon cord, kaizen, and continuous process improvement (CPI) have historically been associated with the empowerment and education of employees.

Employees engage with the process of taking ownership for solving problems within their own sphere of influence. Typically, there is also a focus on working within teams. In this spirit, the boys and their mother gather in the backyard to interact as a team and solicit everyone's input in an effort to solve the problem.

CPI can promote independence and decentralized problem solving in an organizational setting. Educated, empowered employees feel a sense of ownership regarding their own equipment and processes and understand how their efforts are connected with the larger organization. They can often more effectively solve problems on their own or in teams. In doing so, they create new sources of value, both for themselves and for the organization as a whole.

Recall our example from the "Zeke's Tree" story of the equation that describes the effectiveness of process improvements:

$$E = Q \times A$$

By involving Jackson and Wyatt in the decision-making process, Rebecca has both increased the likelihood of success and aided in the children's own problem-solving independence.

BRAIN PLAY

1. Does "pulling an andon cord" always result in increased engagement? Under what conditions is it important to empower employees with the ability to "pull an andon cord"?
2. What are the steps that an organization should take to begin increasing its engagement levels?
3. Think about a situation in your personal or professional life where establishing a system for group review would be appropriate. Briefly describe the implementation steps.

CHAPTER 18

Putting It All Together

CHLOE MANAGES THE FAMILY BUSINESS

Jennifer Anderson and Chloe Adams, old friends from college, sat in the five-star dining room of the Walden-Aster Hotel. While the two women talked, Guinevere, Chloe's toddler, sat beside them in a high chair and pulled apart a succulent beignet. The women enjoyed she-crab soup as they chatted.

Chloe Adams, mother of three, catches up with Jennifer Anderson, an old college friend, over lunch. While discussing her family, Chloe mentions the ways in which she, her husband, and their three children have been working on improving their processes to benefit family life.

As you read Chloe's story, think about the parallels between her private and professional lives.

Jennifer: So how are things at home?

Chloe: Well, it's been a mixed bag. It's a lot of work keeping up with three children while Dylan tries to organize his schedule. We implemented this online scheduling system that we can both look at and post things to. A lot of his work is electronic, so it made sense to try it out. It's hard enough juggling kids of different ages—managing your own life and marriage as well makes it even harder.

Jennifer: Have you changed anything?

Chloe: I rearranged the laundry room, and we organized the girls' playroom. I joined a carpool, and that lets me spend a little more time with the baby in the morning.

Jennifer: Your job seems harder than mine. That's a lot of improvement projects at once.

Chloe: Oh, I don't know about that.

Jennifer: I guess what I'm saying is, everyone wants to change something about their lives. We do what we can while our choices accumulate, and then we end up where we are today.

Chloe: I suppose. But if everyone is always experiencing some level of discontent, then why isn't everyone engaged in changing some aspect of their lives all the time?

Jennifer: It's the level of dissatisfaction that matters, I think. Whenever you change something, you're going to experience loss for a period of time while you adjust. The promise of the change has to outweigh the cost of the loss. The loss could be the loss of power, prestige, money, time, or stability—or the perception of stability, anyway. I think that even when we assume our systems are stable, they're not. It's a matter of degree.

Chloe: Wow, Jennifer. That's deep.

Jennifer: Deep thoughts are my specialty.

Chloe: So I guess you could say that the promise of the changes in our family outweighed the costs associated with the loss. For instance, we started this whole scheduling and improvement project at home because we realized that something had to give. Dylan was always working, never able to make it home for dinner. As a self-employed executive recruiter, after-hours networking was something he invested in heavily for the first few years. He was always meeting clients while I was home eating with the girls. It got to the point where we knew we had to do something drastic because we simply didn't have enough time together as a family or with each other.

Jennifer: That sounds terrible.

Chloe: Implementing the schedule system has actually brought us closer together. Dylan's a devoted husband and father. There was never a question that we would find a way to dig ourselves out of the hole we realized we were in.

Jennifer: So how did you do it?

Chloe: We started with our first goal: three nights a week scheduled for a family dinner. We found it was really important to set a goal and establish a metric. That was our top-line metric—family meals.

Jennifer: What I learned in business school about change management was that for the change to occur, not only does the promise have to outweigh the cost, you need three other things. First, you have to be dissatisfied with the current state. Second, you have to have a vision for the desired future state. Third, you need systems and processes in place to effect and monitor the change. I've learned that the extent of a change—although you could never really quantify this—is a function of each of these three elements. You and Dylan had the desired state of spending more time together as a close family unit, and you measured and monitored that by scheduling the nights in a week your family has dinner together. I think it's brilliant. You two make a good team.

Chloe: I agree, but remember, the whole family played a role in this change. The girls are now more organized. They understand that packing their lunches and laying their clothes out the night before with their daddy—one of Dylan's changes— has a direct effect on how many nights a week Dylan can be home for family dinner.

Jennifer: That's amazing.

Chloe: It sounds crazy, but even Guinevere gets it. For example, she helps keep her toys clean, even though she's not even 2 years old. When we organized the playroom together, each girl got to choose which toys she wanted to keep. Guinevere has two or three bins that are full of just her toys, and we help her put them back in when she's done.

Jennifer: Sounds like a good example of systems thinking.

Chloe: What do you mean by systems thinking?

Jennifer: It's a term that's used in a lot of corporations and business schools. The idea is to think of the company and all its processes as parts of one organism. Companies exist in contexts—social, governmental, economic, and environmental—and the ways a corporation conducts business has an effect on each of these systems.

Chloe: But I don't see how the choice a corporation makes is anything like Dylan making it home for dinner on time.

Jennifer: What I'm hearing is that the actions of each member of your family have an effect on whether or not you achieve your goals. It's a system.

Chloe: That sounds very philosophical. I gravitate toward the practical—the "how" of a situation. Problem solving. I'm not sure how you put that into practice in a situation like mine. The most useful framework for me to think about this process has been to look at it as a group working together rather than as me just giving orders.

Jennifer: That's a challenge I have at work, too. I'm responsible for my division's bottom line. If people working under me don't perform or produce, it reflects on me. But it's hard to toe the line between correcting what I see as "wrong" behaviors and spending my time walking around and motivating them to improve their performance themselves.

Chloe: I can see how you might feel like a mom, always having to step in and do it yourself!

Jennifer: I try not to do that. I try to let people make their own mistakes.

Chloe: Well, yes, of course.

Jennifer: How do you motivate your team when you feel like you're doing everybody else's job?

Chloe: Let's take Dylan's new role at home. We figured that if he packs the girls' lunches with them and helps them lay out their clothes, then this accomplishes three important things. It gives the girls and their father a chance to interact. It helps with the morning routine and gets us out the door 20 minutes faster. And it means I have about 30 minutes to myself each evening while he's doing that chore, which lets me sort mail, keep up with our bills, and get dinner on the table faster.

MT '11

Jennifer: Just that one action has a cascading positive effect on the whole system.

Chloe: But despite the benefits, Dylan is still getting used to it. He's not home in time every night and doesn't want to do it when he gets home after dinner. So there's some resentment on my part when I have to step in.

Jennifer: Sure—I can't stand having to roll up my sleeves and help someone on my team with their reporting or something else they can't complete. But it has to be done, and there's always a legitimate reason why they can't finish on time. So I have to do it anyway, as much as I would rather focus on what I think of as "my" work.

Chloe: I guess it's your job to help out your team. I mean, you're all in it together. So I can see why you would need to help out the people who work for you, even when it's not your job.

Jennifer: And it's the same with your family. If Dylan's tired when he gets home, it might not be because he just doesn't want to help you, or he doesn't understand how valuable that is. Maybe he's just exhausted.

Chloe: You're right. You know, there's something else I've noticed. Dylan is much happier when he can come up with ideas himself or step into a new role voluntarily. Now I realize what a huge difference my presentation makes. If I ask him questions and then step back to give him the space to answer them, he responds differently than if I just tell him what I want. I was used to doing that before, not because I wanted to order him around, but because it seemed more efficient. My aunt always told me, "No man can read your mind." I took that to mean that I would be better served by telling Dylan what I wanted. But being direct isn't always the answer. I get much better results when I ask questions and take the time to involve him.

Jennifer: It's like that at work, too. People in general like to know that you respect them and their opinions. But there's a balance. You also have to expect the highest level of performance a person is capable of.

Chloe: What's the secret?

Jennifer: Part of it is transparency and using metrics that everyone understands—metrics that are directly tied to the performance of the business. I love your metric: family dinners. It's a great measurement of family connection, and if you weren't doing a whole lot of other things right, dinner wouldn't be coming together for you. Everyone knows his or her role in making that happen. So a failure in the system is easily seen and addressed.

Chloe: That's true. Last week Dylan missed a planned dinner. It was easy to ask him why without sounding accusatory. I was able to ask him neutrally because we've both been working on this together, and he understood that I only wanted to help.

Jennifer: Oh? What did he say?

Chloe: He said that he had been late on some billing and had to stay and finish it. He then explained that he was upgrading his billing system so it would be faster. He had already figured out how to eliminate, or at least reduce, the number of times he wasn't home for that reason in the future.

Jennifer: That sounds promising.

Chloe: Well, I do think it helps to have a metric that everyone understands, and to be transparent, so no one feels like the guy working next to him is being treated differently.

Jennifer: Exactly. In production facilities, we display large charts that show performance by sector and associate. It means that everyone can see how everyone else is doing. It's clear, and it's all based on the same standards and measurements.

Chloe: You know, when we started this whole family project, it was so encouraging. We were motivated and saw the potential for a lot of positive change, all at once. But when we did the work it takes to make the changes happen, it started to become exhausting. We always had to prioritize this project over that project because of restrictions on money or time. It didn't happen like we planned it.

Jennifer: I hate to keep comparing your situation to mine, but that's just like business too. There are always limited resources. There's an art to looking at a business as a total system—running the numbers to help you narrow down the best places to put your time and money—and then using your intuition to help you prioritize based on the market or some other factor you can't put your finger on.

Chloe: Another part of this process improvement program is the constant pressure to outdo yourself. You make a few easy changes that obviously need work, and you start to feel really good. Then life happens, and you see all these other changes that you need to make, and they all cost something. Then the changes you made initially might start to slip. It can be really upsetting, and there's this tendency to feel like you're standing still, or, on a bad day, as if you're not making any difference. But that's not true. And then the kids get four or six months older and everyone's needs shift again. So then you have to rethink all your processes all over again!

Jennifer: Seriously, I feel like my business changes every four or six months, too. The change could be brought on by new technology or a new competitor entering the market. Something as simple as a fluctuation in a foreign exchange rate can completely upend your business, even if all your debt is fixed. Life changes and brings you new things to deal with all the time. But the more you engage with the process, the more capable you are of meeting change head-on, and the more conscious you become of the systems that make up your business—which ones have some give and which need fairly strict parameters to run successfully.

Chloe: You're completely right. I'm constantly taking inventory of my life, my home, my children, my marriage, and my career in ways that I never had time to do before. The more I do it, the better I get. Projects with a more long-term payoff have had a chance to emerge now that the short-term problems have been tackled. If I were a company, I'd have more resources to devote to activities like marketing, training, and strategy. Wait—that's funny ... because Dylan said something the other day about wanting to go back to school to earn an executive MBA.

Jennifer: Really? Never would have guessed that! But I can see how it would be beneficial for his career.

Chloe: Yes, he said something while I was cooking dinner the other day, and I asked him if we could put off the conversation until we had a few more months of this process improvement lifestyle under our belts. I said that the family comes first, and then we can start reaching out in other ways. Now that I think about it, though, Dylan's going back to school would be like investing in infrastructure or training an employee base with new skills—to use your metaphor of the family as a company. If we can afford it, maybe we should do it.

Jennifer reached over and stroked one of the ringlets on Guinevere's head as the child played happily with the toys Chloe had brought for her. Then it was quiet as Jennifer and Chloe concentrated on their desserts.

LEADING STRATEGIC CHANGE
IN A FAMILY SETTING

CHANGE MANAGEMENT

A prerequisite for change is that the promise or potential benefit of the change needs to outweigh the cost of generating and sustaining that change. Three elements are necessary for the change to occur. First, there must be sufficient dissatisfaction with the current state. Second, there must be a clearly defined vision for the future that includes a way to measure progress toward that vision. Third, systems and processes must be in place to effect and monitor the change. The scale and degree of the change—although it could never really be quantified—is a function of each of these three elements.

Lean Takeaways

The success of any Lean journey depends on developing and inspiring the people who are part of that process. All the kanbans, XmR charts, and value stream maps in the world can't create success without the engagement and education of the people involved. Top-line metrics keep people focused on the same things when decisions are made in an empowered, decentralized environment where individuals and teams at the shop floor level are encouraged to take informed action. The role of the Lean leader is to educate, inspire, and be a repository of success stories.

Ask, "What's possible?" The successful Lean leader doesn't need to know all the answers—he or she needs to be able to engage the people who do know. Empowerment, encouragement, and motivation are all important elements of a successful Lean conversion.

Just as with the stories of Zeke and Jackson and Wyatt, the concept of $E = Q \times A$ can be useful here. Because Chloe intentionally involves her family members in her efforts and spends time learning about their needs and objectives, she increases their level of acceptance as well as the likely quality of the solution she seeks.

EMPLOYEE DEVELOPMENT

Chloe discusses the ways in which she and her family have approached employee development as part of their comprehensive change management strategy. Dylan is considering going back to school, and Chloe, while still at home with their three children, is learning about team dynamics and effective management. Not all development needs to occur in the professional sphere or in a publicly recognized forum in order to be valuable.

An educated, competent, engaged workforce can become part of an organization's competitive advantage. Employee development is a leadership choice that can be linked to the value proposition, just like every other operations management decision. Historically, organizational development and employee education have been thought of as "nice extras" that some companies might offer as a part of a benefits package. Another way of looking at organizational development is as a partnership between the employee and the organization. A partnership orientation supports the view that aligned, targeted employee development helps the organization become more competitive in the marketplace. Education builds capability that makes the organization stronger and more flexible. An educated workforce that is committed to continuously growing and developing can become one of the critical factors in an organization's success.

EMPLOYEE BUY-IN

What can we learn from Chloe and Jennifer's conversation about Chloe's improvement goals at home:

- Employee engagement?
- Employee development and education?
- Change management and building consensus?

"What's in it for me?" employees ask. This question is commonly abbreviated as *WIIFM*. Common goals, top-line metrics, and transparency are all helpful in orienting everyone around a desired outcome. It helps people see what's expected or needed from them. Some organizations take this a step further by changing the way they relate to *all* stakeholders, whether external or internal. These organizations move from a stance of "either/or" to embracing a "both/and" orientation.

Buy-in is a concept that builds upon the discussion above regarding employee development. Buy-in and engagement occur when the relationship between employer and employee is viewed as a voluntary partnership by both parties, and there is agreement regarding what constitutes a desired outcome and how that outcome will be measured.

No one truly owns anything unless they discover it themselves. When Chloe realizes that asking Dylan questions instead of making statements produces better results, she practices engagement and buy-in. Dylan comes to his conclusions on his own, and Chloe notices that this creates a more effective result.

Chloe also learns that thinking less about "her" work than about working toward a *team contribution* is beneficial because it allows her to consider her team member's performance from their point of view. Considering her teammate's viewpoint helps her to be more tolerant of perceived inequality and to discover more about the situation. Dylan is late one night to a family meal because he spent extra time at the office implementing a new billing system—a system that he hopes will allow him to spend even more time at home in the future. By asking questions and retaining her objectivity, Chloe allows herself to consider her teammate's point of view. The trust between them—as well as the transparency and clearly defined group metrics—is what makes the difference in the *acceptance* of the change.

Chloe and Jennifer also discuss the balance of responsibility for investment in change between the employer and employee. This is a large part of WIIFM. It is just as destructive for an employer to feel disconnected from employees as it is for employees to feel passive regarding their own development. A critical part of the core purpose for engaging in change management, kaizen, CPI, and development activities is to *empower* employees to more actively participate in their own careers. These frameworks use tools like transparent metrics, as well as systems and processes designed to support and measure progress toward the desired future state. They also promote a sense of partnership and trust among an organization's senior leadership and all employees. All stakeholders agree on a roadmap for success that aligns everyone's efforts and encourages (or even requires) everyone to contribute.

Chloe and Jennifer both describe times when they have been asked to step in and help a teammate (whether a direct report or a family member) who is unable to complete their task. The women report that most of the time, doing so helps to promote a sense of solidarity among the team and keeps them connected with any help their teammates might need in the future. There is certainly a fine line between doing an employee's job for them and partnering with them to understand what might jointly be accomplished to support future improved productivity. Partnership involves building trust and helping each party understand their WIIFM.

DESIGNING A ROBUST PROCESS

The concept of a robust process was described in "Bob's A-Maize-ing Popcorn" in Chapter 11. A robust process is less susceptible to the effects of variability and external shocks. It is the cookie dough that produces great cookies regardless of how much the temperature of the oven fluctuates. Hot, cold, or hot and cold together—those cookies will always turn out great.

The concept of a robust process is also important to Chloe and Jennifer in their improvement efforts. Chloe is in the process of building her family, and Jennifer is in the process of building her business. Both women use leadership and the techniques of utilizing a future-state vision to guide their respective ongoing change processes. As this change process unfolds, each woman seeks to improve her internal processes and capabilities so they become more robust—that is, less susceptible to the onslaught of a normal range of environmental factors.

How do businesses make decisions about whether or not a "disruption" should be acted upon, and if so, by what means? What are the conditions that might prompt an organization to focus its process improvement activities inward rather than outward? Part of the answer to these questions lies in the degree to which a process is affected by the disruption and the degree to which an organization believes that it can exert control over the external event or perceived disruption. There is a risk-versus-return aspect to making this decision. Sometimes the

best approach is an internal adjustment—the market is changing, perhaps, and we need to change with it—and sometimes it's best to sort
out an external response, such as working with suppliers to prevent
the potential loss of a particular sourcing contract. Regardless of the
approach that is taken, this is a strategic choice and it can be helpful
to consider a problem from both positions before sorting out the best
course of action.

BRAIN PLAY

1. What else can Chloe and Dylan do to sustain their momentum? Are three family dinners a week the best metric for
   success? Why or why not?
2. How could a politician such as a president, governor, or
   mayor use these principles to achieve significant change?
   Which of these principles is most important? What are the
   barriers to success?
3. Think about a situation in your personal or professional life
   when you have been included in both a successful and an
   unsuccessful period of change. Can you make any observations about factors that might have contributed to the success or failure of these experiences?

EPILOGUE

In this book, through the experiences of Missy, Erika, Todd, Chloe, David, Theron, and many other characters, we demonstrated how to apply the principles of Lean operations management in everyday life. After each story, we described the relevant generalizable principles, and through brain play questions we challenged you to apply these principles to your own personal and business-related situations. In this manner, our goal was to help you build better judgment and decision-making power. When you can see and recognize that something can be better, and you are familiar with the tools that are available to improve the situation, then you can take action.

None of the concepts presented in this book was rocket science, none of the tools required solving a numeric equation, and none of the solutions was technology based. We did not use these types of analytics. This book is a testament to our view that Lean is *common sense, vigorously applied*.[1] Instead, we advocate the use of easy visual management tools and a bias for simplicity. We believe that in doing so, there are huge benefits to be gained, not only in people's private lives but also in their businesses.

We like to say that "operations management starts at home." When you use your own life and the areas over which you have direct control to begin experimenting with the techniques in this book, you can customize your approach on many levels and quickly build experience and judgment. The accessible nature of aspects of your life that you most closely control can allow you to set priorities in both funding and sequencing—you choose how to begin and which form of muda to tackle next. You can also use a rapid-cycle experimentation format, testing new ideas, monitoring results, and adjusting on the fly. By practicing these approaches at home, you will quickly see an impact on

---

[1] Attributed to Larry Culp, CEO of Danaher Corporation.

your personal productivity. Be prepared to reinvigorate your life with the resources and time you free up as a result of your efforts!

To start, choose the concepts that you think will help you address a pressing problem, either at work or at home. Implement a small change that caught your eye from the book, and observe the results. Over time, you will become adept at recognizing waste and thinking through which concepts might help to eliminate it. Recognizing waste is always the first step.

We've assembled a short list of advice for the first-time or veteran process improver:

- Don't let perfect get in the way of better. Momentum is far more important than being right.
- Stay the course if you don't see the progress you want right away. Don't get discouraged. If things don't seem to be going well, back up and reconsider, but press on.
- Lean is the only race you lose by finishing. It's the *relentless pursuit* that matters. Your goal is not to improve; your goal is to improve the process of improving.
- Some people equate Lean with laying people off. In most scenarios, people can be redeployed. This can have the dual result of repositioning your company for growth and staffing that growth at the same time.
- It's the people! Your goal must be to develop your team and to empower them to be part of the improvement process.

The key to Living Lean is learning to ask, "What's possible?" The successful Lean leader doesn't need to know all the answers—but he or she needs to be able to engage the people who *do* know. Empowerment, encouragement, and enthusiasm are all important elements of a successful Lean conversion. Lean is a balance between being able to envision what *might* be possible and understanding how to apply the concepts and techniques that can move an environment from *what is* toward *what might be*.

You can't do this on your own. It involves the engagement of your friends, family, and coworkers—so share the stories, and share your own successes. Just as Chloe said in the final story as she discussed her approach to working with her family to improve their lives, it's important to allow your colleagues and family members to come to their own conclusions. People are almost always the key to the change. As much as operations management is about inventory and machines, at the end of the day, those things are just there to support the people—who in turn support and provide value to your customers.

Indeed, working with your customers to create improvement solutions is one of the best things you can do. Being in touch with what your customers want allows you to see waste from their perspective, which keeps your efforts aligned with the customer-defined value proposition. Going to the gemba—the physical site of the need for improvement—is an important part of being present and able to sense the types of improvement techniques that might be most beneficial.

In practice, Lean should support relevance and connection between customers, suppliers, and businesses. It should be used as a means of communicating across boundaries. Lean should support an ongoing assessment of the value creation process, from end to end, within an organization—be that organization a business or a family. Lean should always include significant coordination with other people.

All the characters in our stories saw improvement. Their goals varied, and were not all limited to cost savings. Erika wanted to find the right pair of shoes in the morning, Theron wanted his customers to experience efficient service as they enjoyed his coffeehouse, Todd wanted to spend more quality time with his children, and Brad and Gina wanted to always have the right baby care products when needed. While not every Lean project needs to save money, cost savings are almost always a byproduct of Lean done well. Applied Lean concepts can result in lower costs, higher quality and delivery, and ultimately more flexibility.

Please share your success stories with us at #leananthology. We are always in *relentless pursuit* of new and ingenious applications of the Living Lean techniques in everyday life. Good luck!

INDEX